JUST CALL ME BOB

JUST CALL ME BOB

THE WIT AND WISDOM OF ROBERT W. FUNK

Edited by Andrew D. Scrimgeour

POLEBRIDGE PRESS
Santa Rosa, California

Cover and interior design by Robaire Ream

Cover: Robert Funk, Delphi, Greece, 2000. Photograph by Char Matejovsky. Used by permission.

Library of Congress Cataloging-in-Publication Data

Funk, Robert Walter, 1926-2005.
  Just call me Bob : the wit & wisdom of Robert W. Funk / edited by Andrew D. Scrimgeour.
     p. cm.
  ISBN-13: 978-1-59815-005-6 (alk. paper)
  1. Christianity. 2. Theology. 3. Funk, Robert Walter, 1926-2005. I. Scrimgeour, Andrew D., 1945- II. Title.
  BR123.F933 2007
  230--dc22
                                        2007040538

*A*nother dawn, leaden
and cold. I am up
alone, searching
again for words
that will make
some difference . . .

"Words"
—Philip Levine

Contents

Acknowledgments

I have been admirably assisted in this project by some very able people. Isaac Kim, my research assistant, assembled the entire Funk corpus for me. Lois Sechehay and Kathy Juliano of the Interlibrary Loan Department of the Drew University Library provided impeccable, gracious service—a quality for which their department is well known. Lane C. McGaughy of Willamette University reviewed the entire manuscript and saved me from many an error. Lee Masters at Westar Institute caught many mistakes as the consummate proofreader. Char Matejovsky, my editor at Polebridge Press, was an advocate of this project from its inception, assisted me in tasks large and small over the past two years. She and Kent Horsley, independent of each other, suggested the title for the book. Brandon Scott brought his critical eye and generous spirit to many aspects of the book. Roy Hoover, Brandon Scott, and Char Matejovsky provided most of the quips. David Herrstrom, Ernest Rubinstein, Dorothy Scrimgeour, Drew Scrimgeour, and Meghan Scrimgeour trimmed and refined my prose, reminding me that my computer came complete with a delete button.

I owe a special debt to William J. Hynes, president of St. Norbert College, who long ago at Regis University taught me how to break big projects into smaller ones and to look for ways to make the interim steps significant. Without that advice, it would have never occurred to me to create this volume en route to writing a biography of Robert Funk.

Introduction

Who Was Robert W. Funk?

- A major scholar of the New Testament (1926–2005).

- Best known as the Founder of the Jesus Seminar, an independent think tank of scholars that freed biblical scholarship from its isolation in universities and seminaries and placed it on the front pages of the newspapers and magazines of America. Few scholarly endeavors in the field of religion have received such sustained public scrutiny.

- Believed that it was ethically abhorrent for biblical scholars not to be willing to say clearly to the general public what they discussed openly in their classrooms and seminars.

- Earned his Ph.D. at Vanderbilt University. Won honors as a Guggenheim Fellow and Senior Fulbright Scholar.

- Taught at Texas Christian University, Harvard Divinity School, Emory University, Drew University, Vanderbilt Divinity School, and co-founded the Department of Religion at the University of Montana.

- Wrote many books including *Language, Hermeneutic, and Word of God* (1966), *Jesus as Precursor* (1975), *Parables and Presence* (1982), *The Poetics of Biblical Narrative* (1988), *The Five Gospels: The Search for the Authentic Words of Jesus* (with Roy W. Hoover and the Jesus Seminar, 1993), and *The Acts of Jesus: The Search for the Authentic Deeds* (with the Jesus Seminar, 1988), *Honest to Jesus: Jesus for a New Millennium* (1996) and *A Credible Jesus* (2002), as well as two Greek grammars.

- Through his work, revolutionized the study of the historical Jesus and the parables of Jesus.

- Led and reorganized the Society of Biblical Literature, the oldest learned society in North America, as its Executive Secretary.

- Founded two presses—Scholars Press, serving a consortium of learned societies including the Society of Biblical Literature and the American Academy of Religion, and Polebridge Press—the publication arm of the Westar Institute and the Jesus Seminar.

- Launched two major journals, *Semeia: An Experimental Journal for Biblical Criticism* and *Forum,* as well as a magazine for the general public, *The Fourth R: An Advocate for Religious Literacy.*

Six Reasons Why You Should Read This Book

1. You will meet a biblical scholar who was passionate about his work and its implications for a credible faith in the twenty-first century.

2. You will learn the difference between telling the truth and skirting the truth.

3. You will learn why scholars, students, clergy, and the general public, alienated from their churches, found haven and hope in Funk's work.

4. You will learn why Funk upset many scholars.

5. You will learn why Funk upset many clergy.

6. You will never again lack for something to say when you shake hands with a minister or priest after a Sunday service or at a cocktail party.

Keeping Jesus Awake

Over the past two years I mined the extensive writings of Robert W. Funk for the nuggets that fill this volume. My digging took me to dozens of essays and books. Whether I was delving into a technical article, a letter to *Time* magazine, or a videotaped lecture, I was struck, not only by the power of Funk's thought, but by the freshness of his language.

He had a knack for taking a concept and making it understandable, compelling, vivid, and, more often than not, memorable. His word clusters light up the page like billboards after dark. He seems constitutionally incapable of being dull. You do not need caffeine to stay awake through a Funk performance.

Working my way through the Funk *oeuvre* reminded me of a string of experiences from my Denver days in the early 1980s. I often visited Ronald Sleeth, a seminary professor, in his cramped office at the Iliff School of Theology. Even though I braced myself each time I walked in, I was startled by what I saw. There was Jesus, sound asleep behind Sleeth's desk. Sleeth taught homiletics, the art of preaching, and was well known for a full-color, life-size mural that dominated one wall. It depicted parishioners at a Sunday morning worship service as viewed by a minister or priest standing in the pulpit. Jesus sat in a place of honor in the front pew—sound asleep. You could almost hear him snoring. It was a powerful message for Sleeth's aspiring preachers.

Funk would have loved that mural. Throughout his career he railed against scholars who had become so specialized that they only wrote for each other and were incapable of engaging the public beyond the university. For him, true scholars were those who had learned to speak to a general audience. The ability to tack between specialist peers and ordinary citizens, not a bibliography of pedantry, was the telling mark of the educated person. His hero was William Rainey Harper, first president of the University of Chicago, who, in stark contrast to contemporary purveyors of insular scholarship, famously urged his faculty to speak to and write for a broader public. In Funk's own words, it is the judgment of most promotion and tenure committees that "if a work is well written and elicits a broad readership, if a sentence is understandable, if students actually learn, then that scholarship cannot be very profound."

Clergy were not exempt from Funk's criticism. He understood why Jesus would sleep through the typical Sunday homily. In his opinion, too many sermons were divorced from current biblical scholarship, the scientific world view, and the perennial questions of meaning. Church leaders "have suppressed the questions people are asking" and do not want "to disturb the faith of simple believers, as though the suppression of knowledge can somehow advance the faith. In so doing, they are postponing a rendezvous with the issues that are emptying the churches and crippling the intellectual integrity of the Christian tradition." Funk often spoke with sadness about former students returning to visit him and telling him that, try as they might, they could not find churches in their cities that were rooted in the scholarship they had learned as undergraduates.

He is often witty and used humor to good advantage. Funk discovered that Jesus enjoyed bringing a chuckle to the crowds: "Jesus' saying about giving up one's shirt to go with a coat claimed under the law would have been a howler in a two-garment society." Funk never used humor to belittle others. Rather, "humor . . . is primarily a good laugh at self-importance, at one's own foibles, at pomposity, at pretension, at arrogance. As a consequence, I have never been prompted to laugh with Jerry Falwell; I am always tempted to laugh at him. That is not the best form of humor."

While Funk was serious about his work, he did not take himself too seriously. He would not allow major achievements of his collaborative scholarship to become icons of veneration. He insisted that even the monumental *Five Gospels: The Search for the Authentic Words of Jesus*, a best seller, was a provisional report, not a reference work for the ages, but one ever ripe for correction and revision. On his intellectual quest, he preferred to travel lightly with just a pup tent, a few provisions, with no household gods.

Much of Funk's writing has a conversational quality. That was not accidental. He was always *talking* about his work with scholars, students, and anyone who was interested. Conversation was not merely communication but a critical form of inquiry. While talking, he was working—trying out ideas, getting reactions, hearing the proposals of others, testing expressions of thought. He never worked in isolation. When he left university life and no longer had colleagues in offices down the hall, he simply assembled scholars from across the continent for major collaborative projects. That was part of the genius of The Jesus Seminar and the Westar Institute. And that work had a very public audience, for the semi-annual sessions of The Jesus Seminar were conducted in front of an audience that could then freely engage the scholars during breaks and meal times. Reports of the work of The Jesus Seminar were written in a lively style and distributed to the media. For many years Funk conducted a weekly class for people in northern California who were interested in current biblical scholarship and its ramifications for an authentic contemporary faith. Many quotes selected for this volume come from articles that he wrote for *The Fourth R: An Advocate for Religious Literacy*, a magazine devoted to bringing the best of biblical scholarship to a general audience. Those essays were shaped in verbal exchanges and retain a lively informal style.

He was ever the teacher, committed to clarity of language. He took a dim view of scholars who sought mainly to impress their audiences with erudition rather than with lucidity and cautioned that abstruse vocabulary should not be mistaken for high scholarship.

Aphorisms and parables were his delight. Not only were they his scholarly preoccupation for over forty years, they sprouted effortlessly whenever his fingers touched his keyboard. In the middle of an executive report to a learned society, a genre known to produce yawns, the reader finds a gem like: "The standard bureaucrat confuses the habitual 'no' with the power to discriminate." Or an essay on parables glistens with: "The makers of genuine parables should be known by the complaints they precipitate, not by the moralisms they propagate."

Closely allied with these witty compressions of wisdom was Funk's penchant for creating lists of theses—short, trenchant statements that provoked thought, summarized an argument, or suggested a course of action. They often were the nub of an article, and, in the case of *Honest to Jesus*, the grand finale. "The Ten Words of Jesus" and "Twenty-One Theses" are classic examples.

The authentic Funk was aphoristic, witty, and aural. He is also passionately direct. He does not mince words. He does not dodge the controversial issues. In his unpublished memoir, he speaks of finally finding full freedom of expression once he was independent of the academic campus. "Suddenly it became acceptable to say what was on one's mind, without equivocation; at that moment it became unacceptable to dissemble." I had not known the word "dissemble" until I heard Funk use it, and it appears often in his writing. Dissembling—obfuscating the truth, dodging or disguising the truth, the art form of the White House press conference—was anathema to Funk. His prose is nothing if not candid, and he urged his colleagues to court courage in their writing and public speaking.

The danger in creating a book like this is reducing Funk's thought to mere sound bites. But that is always the risk with colorful writing and speaking. Yet if the quotes provoke, challenge, enrage, refresh, delight, or compel the reader to dig deeper into the matter, then Funk would approve. After all, that was his modus operandi. To that end, the source for each quotation is provided at the back of this volume.

I selected the quotes for their pungent quality; they do not by any means represent a comprehensive sampling of Funk's thought. They are simply passages that arrested me as I read. I have arranged them by topic and these headers are meant to be generous bins rather than confining pigeonholes. Many of the snippets can claim citizenship in multiple categories. The oldest quotes date from 1964 and the most recent from 2005. Funk was committed to inclusive language, so, like Bernard Brandon Scott in *Funk on Parables: Collected Essays* (Polebridge 2006), I have adjusted some of the earlier texts.

Although there are some intentional sequences to it, the book is not designed to be read systematically. So sample here, sample there, and let Funk draw you into his world of parables with its glimpses of a new reality. I dare say he will keep you awake. And Jesus, too.

High Bridge, New Jersey
July 4, 2007

God

*J*esus experiences God, not as remote from the world, but as everywhere present in the most ordinary events.   2003

Jesus never refers explicitly to God in his twenty-two authentic parables. In his aphorisms, references to God are often to the kingdom of God, which are not references to God as a person or object, but to a sphere of meaning, a storied world. Jesus also alludes to the providence of God, for example, in sayings about good gifts, the lilies of the field, the sparrows and the birds. Unlike Homer, he nowhere depicts God as a player in the human drama. In teaching his disciples to request bread for each day, he was not asking God to drop manna from heaven as in the wilderness, but suggesting that they rely on the largesse of neighbor. God is in the umbra of Jesus' vision: God is implied but not visible, does not appear.   1997

Jesus did not have a doctrine of God; he had only experience of God.   2002

Jesus rejected the deuteronomic thesis that the righteous prosper while the wicked suffer. In the Fourth Gospel, we are told that the man was not born blind because he or his parents had sinned; he was born blind so that light could come into his life. In that gospel, blindness and sight symbolize true and false knowledge. According to Jesus, God causes the sun to shine on both the good and bad; God sends rain on both the just and the unjust. The playing field of life is level.   1996

The old God of Israel was essentially a tribal God. God had chosen this particular people to favor and often intervened in the course of events on their behalf. To be sure, he sometimes intervened to punish them. But the Israelites were bound to Yahweh

3

and Yahweh to them by covenant. The relationship between the two was a distinct disadvantage to the Canaanites, Egyptians, and Babylonians, except that they had their own tribal deities in turn. It was a war of the gods.

Christians inherited this former tribal God, who had been converted to a universal monotheistic God by the great prophets. But the old God had been conceived in the era of absolute monarchies, when emperors and kings had unlimited power. Monarchs demanded constant worship and praise, as tyrants are wont to do. The chief metaphors for Yahweh were derived, as a consequence, from the protocols common to royalty. God was the lord of lords and king of kings, epithets later transferred to Jesus of Nazareth. And the realm where God ruled was called the *kingdom of God.* Our creeds and confessions, psalms and hymns are loaded with language derived from the ancient royal court.

A conflict arises, however, when the old tribal deity, who intervenes in history on a small and often personal scale, is juxtaposed with the universal God of law and order, of justice and fair play, who was introduced by the great prophets of Israel. Yet it is the inflated tribal deity that has survived in Christian tradition: that God answers prayers on behalf of certain petitioners, performs miracles now and again, supplies little banes and blessings to individuals and favored groups, as Don Cupitt has put it.

That God is a relic of the small-scale deity of the earlier layers of the Hebrew Bible. And as a monarch, this deity is subject to flattery and bribes. A God who is discriminatory, inconstant, capricious, or arbitrary is not adequate even for our paltry human sense of justice and fair play. Yet the tribal deity survives in popular and ecclesiastical piety because the large God of physics, biology, astronomy, and philosophy seems too abstract and remote to be influenced and bribed. Yet for us to believe in God, we must have a God who endorses and supports justice for all, impartially, without favoritism, relentlessly, and without fail.   2003

The final nail in the coffin of the old tribal deity is the discovery that belief in God is not the foundation of morality.   2003

We have been slow to conclude that there is no place for a God to dwell "up there" in the far reaches of space and no concept of deity adequate to what we now know of the physical universe. The best we have been able to do is to think God back inside the new physics, the theory of relativity, and quantum mechanics. That has left us with a God who is homeless.   2003

God may continue to be useful as a symbol of transcendence. Transcendence means that God is more than the world. Transcendence means that there is more to the world than meets the eye. Things are not what they seem.   2003

Historical Jesus

*T*he quest of the historical Jesus is a quest in the spirit of Homer's Odysseus and Arthur's knights of the Round Table. It does not involve sailing ships, the one-eyed Cyclops, Sirens, broadswords, and grateful maidens. Yet it is no less a quest story, and it is no less beset by dangers and pitfalls of every kind. The search for the Jesus of history is a quest for the holy grail of truth. 1996

The quest of the historical Jesus is an effort to emancipate the Galilean sage from the tangle of Christian overlay that obscures, to some extent, who Jesus was and what he said, to distinguish the religion *of* Jesus from the religion *about* Jesus. 1996

To describe Jesus is to let him speak for himself, so to speak. But he cannot easily do so from out of and under a long tradition of interpretation that may have muffled his voice. The interpretive enterprise can and must afford, at times, to be hands-off and suggestive rather than didactic and prescriptive. Hence, it seems necessary to let Jesus' real successors discover him to us. When that happens, Jesus arrives, as often as not, as the unfamiliar, or even offensive, precursor, in the guise of a stranger, as one unknown, as Albert Schweitzer once remarked. Congratulations are in order to those who take no offense, as the gospel suggests. 1975

Critical scholars are agreed that the historical figure differs in numerous important respects from the picture painted of him in the four canonical stories. 2002

Individuals and institutions or groups answer the question: Who IS Jesus? Scholars, in contrast, seek to answer the question: Who WAS Jesus? 1992

In order to pursue the Jesus question as a genuine historical question, biblical scholars have had to divorce their work from ecclesiastical and theological control, from the domination of the church. In addition, scholars have had to pry the Jesus question loose from the grasp of the individual, who insists on reading the bible devotionally, without any attention to what these ancient texts meant in their time and place. The strategy of historical scholarship has been to relocate Jesus *way back there*, in his own time and place, far removed from the immediate interests of modern institutions or personal needs. Jesus confronts us as a stranger in the pages of the gospels. . . . He is alien to our way of thinking and living. To recover that stranger is the task of those who have devoted their lives to rediscovering the ancient world through its surviving documents and artifacts.   1992

It may be thought that the first danger to which the quest of the historical Jesus is open is that it will discover a Jesus who is wholly compatible with its active life-world. That threat is ever immanent, but it is not the first danger. The ultimate threat is that such a quest, if executed faithfully, will discover a Jesus that is unpalatable, distasteful, and inimical to the tradition to which he belongs. That is a danger because it will be fundamentally disruptive to the community of faith. On the other hand, the kingdom of which Jesus spoke was fundamentally disruptive to the community of faith to which he addressed his parables. . . . Put theologically, the strength of the tradition lies in its power to invoke its memory against its own proclivity to domesticate the tradition.   1985

David Friedrich Strauss' skepticism did not arise arbitrarily from a willful desire to disbelieve. It was the result of the emergence of an acute historical consciousness, of the desire to know what really happened.   2003

In public controversies in the modern period, the divinity of Jesus is usually made the test of correct belief, particularly on the part of fundamentalists. One is never charged with heresy for not believing in the humanity of Jesus. Yet one of the earliest heresies in the Christian movement was docetism—the view that Jesus only appeared to be human, but was in fact a divine figure in disguise.

Some Docetists held that Jesus miraculously escaped death, that Judas Iscariot or Simon of Cyrene died in his place. Docetism was characteristic of the Gnostics and was vigorously combated by Ignatius and other leaders in the second century.

Taken broadly, the gospels were the counterbalance to a thinker like Paul of Tarsus, for whom the historical Jesus played little role. In modern times, the quest for the historical Jesus has often been resisted or rejected by those for whom Jesus is exclusively a divine figure.   1991

The resolution of the argument regarding the historical Jesus will not take place finally in learned books but in the public market place of real needs and viable ideas.   1999

The discrepancy between the historical Jesus and the picture painted of him in the narrative gospels is a permanent feature of critical scholarship and theology.   2000

We will never be able to recover the precise words of Jesus, whether because he spoke them originally in Aramaic now lost, or because oral transmission has hopelessly obscured them. The best we can hope for is to reconstruct their approximate sense.   1989

Critical Questions

- The interpreter who wants to make claims about Jesus has to declare his or her database: What are the materials, in what sources and in what level of what sources, on which your views are based?
- The interpreter must declare a thesis: What are the fundamental threads of your sketch of the historical Jesus?
- What can be said against your thesis? What evidence is left over that you could not accommodate? Beware of those who can explain everything.
- Does your thesis account for the variety and contradictions that appear to characterize the Jesus tradition at its earliest levels? The ultimate test is whether your thesis will explain how so many diverse views of Jesus arose in such a short span of time.

- Finally, do your conclusions represent religious views you yourself espouse and which you can recommend to your family and friends? Do your conclusions match the creed to which you previously subscribed? If you have answered yes to any of these questions, the chances are you have discovered a Jesus in your own image. A Jesus tailor-made to specifications will not be the historical Jesus, but a fictive Jesus, like the one the evangelists imagined for themselves at the beginning of the era.   1989

Criteria for Determining the Authentic Sayings of Jesus

- Jesus said things that were short, pithy and memorable.

- Jesus spoke in aphorisms—short, pithy memorable sayings and in parables—short, short stories about some unspecified subject matter.

- Jesus' language was distinctive.

- Jesus' sayings and parables have an edge.

- Jesus' sayings and parables characteristically call for a reversal of roles or frustrate ordinary everyday expectations: they surprise and shock.   1990

I share an interest in who Jesus is and especially who he *was*. I am intrigued by the provocative but shadowy figure that one occasionally catches sight of in the ancient gospel texts. In his authentic parables and aphorisms, Jesus provides a glimpse into another reality, one that lies beyond present conceptual horizons. His words and deeds open onto that reality. His vision, in my view, is worth exploring. The Jesus of that alternative world encourages me to celebrate life, to suck the marrow out of existence, to explore, and probe, and experiment, to venture into uncharted seas, without fear of a tyrannical and vindictive God. He does not set limits on my curiosity, or my drive to challenge every axiom. That same Jesus prompts me to give myself to tasks that exceed, even contradict, my own self-interest.   1996

The real reason for rediscovering the historical Jesus is to allow an ancient Jesus to confront the many faces of the modern

Jesus. The Jesus we begin with is the Jesus we have enshrined in our images and creeds, our reconstructions and convictions, our hopes and our fears. The Jesus that lies at the end of the return to Nazareth is someone we do not yet know. Whatever he turns out to be, he will subvert the Jesus we think we know, the Jesus we venerate and cherish. We must be prepared for the potential emotional and intellectual turmoil that discovery will produce. 1996

The Jesus movement was, from the very beginning, in the minds of Jesus' first and most intimate companions, a welter of responses—impulses, convictions, emotions, memories, typifications, practices, false starts, new hopes, struggles for power, and related human reactions. It is possible to isolate many of these tiny blips on the screen of history if we pay sufficient attention to detail and do not let our preconceptions overrule what our texts tell us on their own terms. 1996

If we cannot reach the original, the real Jesus, the true Christianity, what is the purpose of the quest? The answer is worth repeating: The aim of the quest of the historical Jesus is to set Jesus free, to liberate him from prevailing captivities. Truth is a moving target. It is always necessary to remind ourselves that the liberated Jesus will eventually be imprisoned again and reentombed. Then it will be time to start all over again. 1996

Neo-orthodox theologians held that it was impossible to recover the real Jesus owing to the nature of the gospels. They also believed that it was theologically illegitimate to base Christian conviction about Jesus on historical data, inasmuch as those data are never finally fixed: historical scholarship, they argued, can produce only relatively assured results, but the Christian faith requires absolutely reliable foundations. The faith, they insisted, rests on the first confessions of Peter the fisherman and Paul the tentmaker rather than on anything Jesus said or did. And that, they concluded, is the best we can do. 1996

In the Gospel of John, Jesus is a self-conscious messiah rather than a self-effacing sage. In John, Jesus seems to have little concern for the impoverished, the disabled, and the religious outcasts. Although John preserves the illusion of combining a real Jesus with the mythic Christ, the human side of Jesus is in fact diminished. For all these reasons, the current quest for the historical Jesus makes little use of the heavily interpreted data found in the Gospel of John. 1996

Gospel of Jesus, Vision of Jesus

*J*esus fraternized openly and shamelessly with prostitutes, petty tax officials, and other riffraff in violation of the social codes of his day.   1996

The pale, anemic, iconic Jesus suffers by comparison with the stark realism of the genuine article.   1996

Like other exorcists of his time, Jesus had power over what were thought to be demons. He believed the reign of Satan had come to an end and the earth swept clear of demons. The full force of that conviction was not to be realized for more than 1600 years: only then, with no gods, spirits, or demons to offend, the empirical sciences could take their rise.   1996

Jesus' vision . . . was subversive of many aspects of the "they say" reality. And the "they say" outlook eventually smothered Jesus' vision by encasing it in the popular symbolic universe. The vision of Jesus was sucked back into the gravitational field of the paramount reality. But it left some debris of its disruptive presence scattered around in the solar system of its memories.   2003

Jesus enjoined subversive forms of social behavior and practiced those same tenets himself. He justified his thought and behavior as the enactment of his Father's will. He believed the Creator made the world in the shape and with the contours as he mirrors them in his parables and witticisms. He seems never to have considered whether he might be mistaken. But his confidence, as unrelenting as it was, did not make him arrogant. He claimed nothing for himself, asked nothing of his followers that would benefit him. He appears to have followed his own admonition: "the first will be last, and the last first" (Matt 20:16).   1992

The gospel Jesus proclaimed differs in rather remarkable ways from the Jesus pictured in and proclaimed by the canonical gospels—Mark, Matthew, Luke, John. We have distinguished the gospel of Jesus from the Jesus of the narrative gospels. From a larger perspective, the narrative gospels combine the gospel of Paul with the gospel of Jesus.   1993

In a well-ordered society, people know their places. In Jesus' world the few very rich and the many very poor knew their places. The social distance between them was mediated by brokers who dispensed favors bestowed by patrons on compliant peasants and peons. Social stratification was enforced by the purity system, which segregated lepers, women, petty tax officials, demoniacs, cripples, and gentiles.

In the midst of this order, Jesus is socially promiscuous: he eats and drinks publicly with outcasts, yet he does not refuse dinner with the learned and wealthy. He is seen in the company of women in public—an occasion for scandal in his society. He includes children in his social circle and advises that God's domain is filled with them.

It is not just his company at table, it is also what he eats. He eats whatever is set before him, which means that he ignores kosher restrictions. On this point, he acts the pundit: "It's not what goes in that pollutes, but what comes out" (Mark 7:15). (We are left to figure out which orifice of the human body he has in mind.)

Adding these practices up, we see that Jesus was a pronounced social deviant. He did not know his place, and he advised others not to know theirs.   1993

The wall around temples in the ancient Near East—called a temenos—separated priests from worshipers. It defined sacred space and set if off from profane space.

Jesus breached that wall. He believed that not one stone would be left on top of another—a possible reference to the coming destruction of the Jerusalem temple. A temple without a temenos—a church without a chancel, had he been able to foresee the future—means that every person has immediate and equal access to God.

Jesus advises the Samaritan woman at the well that true worshipers will worship the Father without regard to place. Neither Jerusalem nor Gerizim—nor Rome—defines sacred space.   1993

Jesus practiced and advocated an unbrokered relationship to God: for him temple and priests were redundant.   1996

The gospel of Jesus has little in common with what is popularly identified as the Christian gospel.   1993

On the basis of the parables, we might conclude that Jesus rarely spoke about religion at all.   1975

In his brief references to God, Jesus is not adopting a metaphysical creed—or preparing the way for one—but observing the world as he sees it—as though it were in an intensive care unit run by his Father.   1985

A close examination of the aphorisms and parables indicates that Jesus did not speak of himself as the messiah, did not anticipate his own death, did not predict that he would rise from the dead, did not believe he would return as the heavenly son of Adam. We can only conclude that these features are part of the Christian overlay that transformed the proclaimer into the proclaimed.   1993

The narrative gospels are not biographies and the evangelists are not historians. The gospels are religious propaganda and the evangelists are religious propagandists. They had no interest in history, except as that history conformed to ancient prophecies. Their interest was in marketing the messiah. That promotional job would have been easier without the crucifixion, which, after all, was a very unmessianic thing to have happened. The crucifixion was the one indisputable fact that neither they nor their opponents could deny.   1993

Jesus did not ask us to believe that he was the messiah. He certainly never suggested that he was the second person of the trinity. In fact, he rarely referred to himself at all, and when he did only to depict himself as homeless.   1993

Jesus had nothing to say about himself, other than that he had no permanent address, no bed to sleep in, no respect on his home turf. He did not ask his disciples to convert the world and establish a church. He did not believe the world was going to end immediately, unlike John the Baptist, who was an eschatological prophet who expected God to intervene directly in history in the near future. Jesus apparently did not even call on people to repent, and he did not practice baptism. He may have eaten a last meal with the inner circle of his followers, but he did not initiate what we know as the Eucharist. In short, very little of what we associate with traditional Christianity originated with him. 1996

Readers of the gospels speak glibly about the religion of Jesus because his followers created a religion about Jesus. It is not at all clear that religion concerns Jesus. 1975

Jesus is a heroic figure because he has ventured through the apertures of his own parables and aphorisms. 1996

The new Jesus is as frustrating as the old one, only in a different, more immediately relevant way. He tells us to go but won't show us the way; he sets us to tasks for which we have neither the inclination nor the equipment. He introduces us to a realm in which there are no rights, only responsibilities. But this is a society in which there are only rights and no responsibilities. So, this new Jesus lacks widespread appeal.

Americans, John Chancellor opines, used to look up and outward; now they look down and inward. This new Jesus is too optimistic for Americans. He looks up and ahead. Many prefer to hold their heads down, to pursue the inward quest. It is easier and safer. 1993

Jesus has become a more realistic, engaging figure when reclothed in the tattered garments of an itinerant Galilean sage and freed from the panoply of adoration. In that guise he seems to speak more directly and powerfully to a complex world in need of simpler yet profound truths. Nevertheless, his vision has very limited use if not properly understood and translated into strong contemporary idiom. 1999

Jesus of Nazareth would have been no more welcome among the church fathers than he was among members of the Purity Party in his own day.   2000

The gospels can be said to function as a counter-weight to the emphasis on the divinity of Jesus that leads up to the Apostles' Creed. They focus rather on the public life of Jesus.   1991

Jesus denied his followers any sense of or right to Christian "privilege." One can be first only by being last. One can preserve life only by losing it. Like the prodigal, one can come home only by perpetually leaving home.   1996

Jesus' vision consisted not of a new self-understanding but of a new reality-understanding. The reality human beings inhabit—cohabit, actually—is socially constructed, maintained, and transmitted by and through the social structures to which they belong. Jesus broke through the crust of his inherited world and achieved a vision of an alternative reality. He articulated that vision in his parables and aphorisms. His vision consisted of many separate observations on the world around him, which, when taken together, constituted an alternative working world—not a worldview, but a lived horizon of possibilities. He seemed strange to family and friends because his world did not coincide with theirs.   1997

If the gap between the visionary and the average human is wide, the line between the true visionary and the insane is extremely thin.   1997

The gospel of Jesus is not mythological. The major mythic themes of the kerygma and creed are missing from his pronouncements. He does not represent God as intervening directly in history. As the fountainhead of the tradition, the articulated vision of Jesus provides us with a gospel already demythologized.   1997

Reality is fabulous, as Thoreau puts it. When Jesus calls attention to the ordinary—the seed growing, the friend pounding on the door at midnight, two men at prayer—he does not intend that we should think of something else, such as religion, or synagogue, or God. He intends that we should see what he sees, there, in the things themselves. . . . The sacred has come to dwell in the common and ordinary, in the ongoing and repetitious acts of living.   1975

Jesus' language is concrete, vivid, pithy, often humorous, because it indulges hyperbole, paradox, or irony. Jesus employs caricatures: we must therefore be cautious in taking his depictions of opponents at face value. Jesus appears never to have given a direct, unequivocal answer to a question (should we pay taxes or not?), never a literal piece of advice (let the dead bury their dead).   1989

The narrative contexts in which the sayings of Jesus are preserved in the gospels are the creations of the evangelists. They are fictive and secondary.   1989

Jesus' assessment of himself has been a difficult issue for critical scholars. The gospel records do not give us access to Jesus' mind, except indirectly, and early Christian conviction simply overwhelmed the tradition: it made Jesus testify to the status accorded him by believers. In the popular mind, if Jesus did not think of himself as the expected messiah, then he was not. More sophisticated theologians are inclined to the view that if Jesus knew himself to be the messiah, his incarnation would have been a chimera, he would not have been fully human, contrary to the creed, and his acceptance of the cross a sham.   1989

Had Jesus lived in Salem, Massachusetts in the seventeenth century, he would have been accused of witchcraft. For to be demon-possessed means that one operates by means of the powers of darkness. As a consequence, the demon-possessed in Jesus' day were forced to live out in the wilderness, among the tombs, as in the case of the Gadarene demoniac.   1989

Jesus had no idea of founding a new order, social or otherwise, and he did not envision anything like the church that arose in the wake of his death.   1989

Visions come in bits and pieces, in random stunning insights, never in continuous, articulated wholes. That is because visions are more than the sum of their parts. 2002

Jesus' vision did not have to do with lofty theories or grand abstractions. It did not derive from the interpretation of ancient texts. With very few exceptions, Jesus does not appeal to the priesthood, or the temple, or purity distinctions, to the scribes, or to the Torah. 2002

We can think of Jesus as the first standup Jewish comic; he can properly be described as a comic savant—a sage who embeds wisdom in humor; a humorist who shuns practical advice. "If someone sues you for your coat, give him the shirt off your back to go with it." That is not practical advice: to follow it is to go naked. Comic wisdom refuses to be explicit. Yet in the stories he tells, the sage constructs a new fiction that becomes the basis for his or her own action and the action of others. The contours of that fiction are ambiguous in order to frustrate moralizing proclivities; they are also open to multiple and deeper interpretations as a way of keeping them open to reinterpretation in ever new contexts. Our task is to follow their lead and figure out what meaning to give them in our own circumstances. 2002

Wisdom is not concerned with theories of sin and salvation, but with how to cope with life. We have identified Jesus as a sage rather than as a lawgiver or a prophet. 1999

//

Sages often embrace poverty as protection against self-aggrandizement. 2002

Some of his followers got the idea right away. They began to see and act on his vision. But they had difficulty interpreting it for themselves in new situations, and transmitting it to others because it was not prescriptive, codified. It was non-literal. They were puzzled by the irony, paradox, parody, and metaphor. So they converted his insights into things they found more useful: They took his basic insights and adopted tables of received virtue and baptized those virtues as their own. They developed sanctions to enforce those virtues and views. They did so on his authority, now believed to be that of a teacher sent from God. An orthodoxy emerged. By the fourth century, the church's salvation machine was in place. Now converts had to submit to the beliefs and practices of the institution in order to merit salvation. Dissidents were deemed heretics. There was no salvation outside the church. And the kingdom had now been transferred to another world, the world beyond the grave and beyond history. Nevertheless, here and there in the tradition one can catch a glimpse of the original—the powerful poet who broke out of the mold and mounted a challenge to the world. And some still get it, in spite of the obfuscating debris of the orthodox tradition preserved in the New Testament gospels and the creeds.   2002

Jesus speaks and acts on his own authority, on the authority of his vision. He does not quote sources. Unlike other teachers, he does not cite and interpret scripture. He does not footnote his assertions with references to other sages. He does not debate fine points in the law. He is not a scribe, a scholar, by disposition. He is an oral sage, who articulates a vision first of all for himself. He is his own authority in that new world.   2002

It seems clear that Jesus had little use for the temple cult. For him persons had direct access to God without benefit of priest or sacrifice. God did not require brokers. The Jesus movement forgot that basic dictum early on in its development.   2002

The first beatitude is powerful evidence for the secret or hidden nature of God's dominion.

Congratulations, you poor!

God's domain belongs to you!

In Jesus' world, the poor and destitute were quite visible. He is probably congratulating the poverty stricken standing around him. They were being awarded something they did not know they possessed. It probably surprised them. They may have tittered or laughed aloud at the preposterous suggestion that the poor were favorites of God. There is no empirical warrant for the assertion that the poor are blessed. The only warrant is their alleged status in the invisible kingdom of Jesus.

The traditional view was that success in the economic and political world followed upon the correct observation of the covenant and the purity codes. . . . Jesus seems to have been in fundamental opposition to this ancient paradigm when he awards a special place in God's realm to the poverty stricken, the hungry, and the tearful. In effect, he claims that the divine realm is peopled by the poor, the tearful, the hungry, and the persecuted. That claim stands the customary view on its head.   2002

The Jesus of the gospel records is an enigma to us because he belongs to an alien time and place. On the authority of those same records, he belonged to yet another time and place even for his contemporaries; by virtue of his vision he did not belong to their everyday world either. We should not be surprised to learn that the Jesus no one really knows is a subverter of causes. That he tramples with disdain on our saccharine sentiments. That he contradicts the labels we pin on him. That he rejects our honors and adoration. That Jesus, like the real Abraham Lincoln and the real Socrates, floats there in the collective imagination as an elusive but endlessly tantalizing figure who, if liberated, promises to help us discover who we really are and what life is all about.   1996

Neo-orthodoxy limited the significance of Jesus to his death and resurrection and thereby made his life prior to Easter irrelevant to the inauguration of the Christian faith.   1996

God has a preference for the lowly, the poor, the undeserving, the sinner, the social misfits, the marginalized, the humble. I doubt that there is any typification, any generalization, about the words and acts of Jesus in which we can have more confidence.   1996

Because Jesus is confident God will provide and because he is willing to trust human generosity, he strongly recommends celebration. He congratulates the hungry and promises them a feast. Jesus shows up both eating and drinking, and so people call him a glutton and a drunk, a crony of toll collectors and sinners. He advises his critics that the groom's friends can't fast as long as the groom is around. His parables are filled with parties—over the recovery of a lost coin, a lost sheep, a lost son—and Jesus pictures the arrival of God's rule as a dinner party. He is the proverbial party animal. . . .   1996

John the Baptist fasted; Jesus did not. As soon as Jesus was gone, the Christian community reverted to the practice of fasting. 1996

It is the journey and not the arrival that constitutes our salvation. This is the ultimate vision of Jesus.   2002

Parables

*J*esus was an iconoclastic Jewish poet who spoke three languages: Aramaic, Greek, and parable.   1996

His parables and witticisms are a knothole in the cosmic fence that fronts the alternative reality he called the kingdom of God. Through that aperture we get a glimpse of the world as Jesus saw it.   1996

It is not too much to say that the true metaphor reveals a mystery: the mystery of kaleidoscopic reality directly apprehended.   1966

The parables, and to a lesser extent the aphorisms, came to be understood as speech forms characteristic of Jesus. In the case of the parables, it was a form Jesus had not borrowed from his predecessors and a form not easily replicated. Very few sages have achieved the same level of creativity with this particular genre of discourse. Franz Kafka and Jorge Luis Borges are among the few who have mastered the form.   1996

The parable, like other works of art, linguistic and visual, can be defined, but only with considerable loss. To grasp the parable in its fullness means to see what happens when parable occurs, to see what happens in the words themselves and to see what happens within the horizons circumscribed by the parable.   1966

There is no closure for the parables; they are open-ended. They do not teach a lesson; they subvert the world humans adopt as their paramount reality.   2002

In my case, it was the rediscovery of the parables and the significance of non-literal or metaphorical language that had shifted my attention from the strict historical interpretation of biblical texts to the literary dimensions of the Jesus tradition. The language of Jesus, I came to see, was secular, literally non-literal, and comic in mode. I learned this not from biblical studies but from the poets and interpreters of the poets like Amos Wilder. The secularity of Jesus pointed to his basic mission, which, to use the words of Paul Tillich, was to relieve us of the burden of religion. There were no literal terms in the parables; he made it all up. And he poked fun at all forms of piety and pomposity. 2002

Jesus told his parables as though he were hearing them. Rather than making a claim for himself or for his Father, he was allowing himself to be claimed by his vision. 1996

The parable is a fantasy—a fantasy about God's domain, an order of reality that feeds on but subtly transforms the everyday world. It is about an order of reality that lies beyond, but just barely beyond, the everyday, the humdrum, the habituated. In that case, the parable is also an invitation to cross over, to leave the old behind and embrace the new. The ability to cross over will depend, of course, on both the tenacity with which one holds to the inherited scheme of things, and on one's willingness to cut the ties to comfortable tradition. The parable is pitted against the power of the proven. Making the transition under such circumstances does not come easily. 2002

Aphorisms and parables are characteristic of the oral speech of Jesus. 1989

The complaint of many is fully justified: parables are frustrating, if not maddening. 1972

Reduction of the meaning of the parables to a single idea be it eschatological or Christological, is only a restricted form of rationalization. As in the case with the allegory, theological reduction seeks to control the metaphor. . . . The metaphor must be left intact if it is to retain its interpretive power. 1966

The final frustration of rationality is to be wrong while being right, to lose while winning. . . . To have won in reality is to remain bound to the every day world, to daily cares, to be unable to heed the invitation to "go over"; it also means to be imprisoned in the literal. 1975

The secularity of the parables may give expression to the only way of legitimately speaking of the incursion of the divine into history: metaphorical or symbolic language is proper to the subject matter because God remains hidden. 1966

The parable does not direct attention by its earthy imagery *away from* mundane existence, but *toward* it. 1966

The parables simply and artfully call up the "world" in such a way that "anyone who has ears" knows that more is at issue than a piece of change or a doting old father. 1966

Like the cleverly distorted picture puzzles children used to work, the parable is a picture puzzle which prompts the question, What's wrong with this picture? 1966

Parables are language events in which the hearer has to choose between worlds. Those who elect the parabolic world are invited to dispose themselves to concrete reality as it is ordered in the parable, and venture, without benefit of landmark but on the parable's authority, into the future. 1966

Those habituated in the Christian tradition of interpretation (mis)take the parable to be a dispensable ornament for a prosaic point, long ago determined. That makes the tradition swinish. Kafka provides a gentle (because implicit) reminder that the parables of Jesus have been eclipsed by their interpretations. The makers of genuine parables should be known by the complaints they precipitate, not by the moralisms they propagate. 1975

Rhetorical strategies are the means by which writers wink at readers. 2004

The measure of success for a creative writer is commensurate with the degree to which she or he has infringed the semantic compact represented by the dictionary. 1975

The gospel tradition . . . set to work to moralize the parables and aphorisms, to supply them with specific courses of action or thought. And scholars have trotted right along in the footsteps of the evangelists. 2004

Jesus is describing life in Galilee as it may be seen through God's eyes. 2004

In the parables reality is aborning. 1982

In the parables of Jesus, God's imperial rule is offered only for what it is, namely, a venture of faith undertaken on the authority of the parable, in the power of the parable. 1975

The striking feature of the parables is that in them Jesus does not speak about what his first listeners—and his subsequent listeners—expected and expect him to speak about. . . . Jesus does not speak about God in his parables, he does not develop a doctrine of God, he does not speak about himself, he does not proclaim his messiahship, he does not predict his passion and death, he does not claim that he is about to die for the sins of humankind, he does not predict that history will soon end, he does not depict a last judgment, he does not picture supernatural beings, or miracles, or even exorcisms, and he does not commission his disciples to form a church and conduct a world mission. On all these topics of burning interest to people in his day, to his disciples of the second and third generations, and modern readers of the gospels, he was and is simply and startlingly silent. 1975

Jesus is not adopting a metaphysical creed—or preparing the way for one—but observing the world as he sees it—as though it were in an intensive care unit run by his Father. 1975

The proverb and parable do not answer the question: What ought I to do? They bring the hearer into the context of decision and provide him or her with the frame of reference within which decision is to be taken. 1971

There is often a tension between the simple or surface sense of a metaphor or parable and its hidden meaning. Yet in the mouth of Jesus the parable does not create an exclusive mystery circle, to whom alone the secret is revealed. On the contrary, the secret or hidden meaning lies in the parable itself, accessible to lettered and unlettered alike. The only qualification is that the parable must be received on its own terms. 1971

The parable is a looking glass that opens onto a familiar but oddly different world. Alice in Wonderland noticed that the room on the other side of the looking glass was the same as her drawing room, only things went the other way around. She also attempted to see that bit behind the fireplace—oh how she wanted to see *that* bit—and when she did see it she discovered that everything there was as different as possible.

The parables of Jesus look out on the everyday world. Everyone knows what it means to have lost a sheep or a coin, to knock on a neighbor's door at midnight in quest of food following the unexpected arrival of a guest, to sow a field, to have a wayward son, to receive the same wage as those who idled away most of the day in the marketplace, to leaven a loaf of bread, to build a house on the sand, to watch a dishonest accountant feather his own nest: these are things everyone knows and can affirm, "Yes, that's how it is." 1965

The parable refuses to satisfy our lust for rational and moral explanation. It steadily calls our attention to the scene before us, and we, just as steadily, seem preoccupied with what remains hidden.

It is not that we do not want to believe. We want almost fiercely to believe, and for that very reason we ask for authority, for evidence. We are especially prone to demand justification when we have endured the burden and heat of the day, when we were given a first invitation to the banquet but refused, not knowing the circumstances. And because we look away at the dark, we miss what has transpired in the world.

We miss what has transpired because we do not notice that the old world has passed away and a new world has come into being. The parable itself has become a looking glass which opens onto a world under the aegis of grace. It invited us not only to look, but to pass through, to live in a looking-glass house. So obvious an invitation makes skeptics of us all, like the offer of a perpetual winning number at Las Vegas.

Why is it so difficult to hear and see the invitation of the parable and then to accept? In the first place, the parable contradicts our notion of what is really real, of what the *world* is. Why should we concede our view of the world to a fanciful tale? And secondly, we are not prepared to believe that mere words can stand up against the abrasive effect of our own raw experience. Both difficulties attest the root significance of our primal, preconceptual, pre-reflective experience of *world*.   1965

The parable is a picture. It is not a story with a moral, it does not teach this or that, but, like a painting, it invites the hearer to skip the intermediaries, the words and sentences, and rejoin the world of the teller, a world which, through the parable, becomes uttered and accessible. If the parable does not transform our experience of the *world*, it is because we take our experience of the world to be given, to be anchored in things as they really are. In that case, the way Jesus experienced the world and the way we experience it simply stand over against each other. Jesus comes off second best because we regard our view of reality as true.   1965

The pristine grammar of the church is the parable, the similitude, the aphorism— a secular, literal non-literal language, comic in mode.   1968

If we can no longer hear or speak parables, at least we can practice laughing—quietly—at the grand hoax to which we are parties. Perhaps then we will become parables.   1968

The dinner party is . . . a parable of radical inclusiveness.　2002

The older son who stayed at home and tended the ranch did not understand why the prodigal son was treated like royalty (Luke 15:11–32). The difference can be put this way: the older son never left home so he could not comprehend what a homecoming was like; the younger son left home, discovered his alienation, so he returned home with the full knowledge of what it was like to be a son. He accepted the terms of a homecoming.　1992

The church, no less than Israel, is wont to stumble over its hope. It seizes, solidifies, and then takes possession of its hope in the name of divinely certified reality. In so doing, it merely converts the mustard plant back onto a towering cedar. As regards that hope and its encapsulation in the tradition, the parable of the Mustard Seed suggests the following items for reflection:

1. Whatever the Christian hope is, the form of its realization will come as a surprise to all who think they know what it ought to be.

2. The coming of God's imperial rule will disappoint the righteous, but be a source of joy to the religiously disinherited.

3. The certainty of hope is inversely proportionate to the certainty with which the resurrection of Jesus is held to be paradigmatic of the future.

4. The promise of the future is directly proportionate to the degree that one makes no claim upon the future at all.

5. The gift of the future is the gift of gesture: the parable is a gesture toward that 'fabulous yonder' that lies on the other side.

From time to time, one gets a glimpse of that other side from this side, through the looking-glass of the parable. Jesus advances the parable as an invitation to pass through the looking-glass. Permission to pass is granted by nothing more than the parabolic gesture, the sight-enabling word that occurs between and among average human beings.　1975

Jesus was evidently given to caricature and exaggeration. His parables function something like modern cartoons that exaggerate the features of a person or event for the sake of immediate and humorous recognition and to make a point. 1996

The message of the parables and aphorisms is first and foremost the announcement of good news: sinners and outcasts are welcome in God's kingdom; indeed, God's domain belongs to them. The bad news is that those who think they are leading upright lives will be surprised to learn that they have missed the messianic banquet, the great supper, because they were too preoccupied with misleading and deceptive aspects of life. According to Jesus' parables and aphorisms, the social roles—marginal versus respectable—will be reversed: the first will be last and the last first, according to Jesus. 1996

The parable has none of the allegorical transparency of *Pilgrim's Progress*; it is a poor road map for the traveler who has lost his way, particularly when the hour is late. 1975

We should avoid the mistake frequently made in popular biblical interpretations: the interpreter, in a rush to get to the moral of the story, forsakes the text prematurely and hastens to some point previously determined, usually without reference to the story itself. The story then becomes merely the occasion for the interpreter to affirm some conviction previously ascertained on some other basis. Much popular biblical interpretation is of this sort. 1996

The parable is pitted against the power of the proven. 1996

Theses Concerning the
Deeds and Parables of Grace

1. Grace always wounds from behind, at the point where people think they are least vulnerable.

2. Grace is harder than people think: they moralize judgment in order to take the edge off it.

3. Grace is more indulgent than people think: but it is never indulgent at the point where they think it ought to be indulgent.

4. Grace is not something humans can have at all.

5. Grace remains a mystery: it unveils itself as the ground of faith, but evaporates like a mist before the acquisitive eyes of belief. 1966

The parables open onto an alternative reality, or altered frame of reference, or field of reference, to which we have customarily given the term Kingdom of God. 2004

In the kingdom of God, or the divine domain as I now prefer to term it, generosity is the rule, because God is generous. 2004

Divine Domain

*T*he theme of Jesus' public discourse was the kingdom of God or God's domain. God's domain was that region or sphere where God's dominion was immediate and absolute. Jesus believed God's reign to be present but not discernible to ordinary eyes. 1996

God's imperial rule inverts the terms of the sacred and the profane. 1975

In God's domain,

- Help comes from the quarter from which we don't want it.
- Help comes from the quarter from which we least expect it.
- Help always comes as a surprise.
- Help is another name for grace—the grace of the Samaritan who was scandalously generous. 2002

Jesus always talked about God's reign in everyday, mundane terms—dinner parties, travelers being mugged, truant sons, laborers in a vineyard, the hungry and tearful. His language was concrete and specific. He did not cite and interpret scripture. He never used abstract language. He made no theological statements. He would not have said, I believe in God the Father Almighty." Or "all human beings have sinned and fallen short of the glory of God." Or "I think, therefore I am." It never occurred to him to assert that God is love. 1996

Jesus conceived of God's rule as all around him but difficult to discern. God was so real for him that he could not distinguish God's present activity from any future activity. He had a poetic sense of time in which the future and present merged, simply melted together, in the intensity of his vision. But Jesus' uncommon sense of time was obscured and then buried by the more pedestrian conception of John the Baptist, on the one side, and by the equally pedestrian views of the early Christian community, on the other.   1992

Jesus' understanding of God's domain may be summarized as follows:
  (a) Jesus indicated God's imperial rule was present in his own words and deeds.
  (b) Jesus spoke of God's domain as present in the everyday, the mundane.
  (c) Jesus suggested that God's rule was not apparent to most folk.   1992

Jesus seems to have specified certain patterns of behavior that are mandated in God's domain; they are not so much requirements for getting into that empire as they are stipulated codes of behavior for those who choose to live as Jesus himself did.   1989

Jesus' vision of the domain of God is counterintuitive. The divine domain runs counter to recipe knowledge.   2002

In God's domain, all we can rely on is the certainty that things will not be what we expect.   2002

Unlike John the Baptist, Jesus did not call to repentance and consequently did not threaten with the wrath of God.   2002

The rewards that Jesus offers are intrinsic to the deeds for which they are the reward, and the punishment consists in the lack of recognition that one is a child of God.   2002

To be an "insider" in the kingdom one must be an "outsider." That requirement is never rescinded. A sinner is an "outsider" — from the standpoint of those who thought they were insiders. In God's domain, Christians may be insiders but they are without privilege. Christians or insiders are never superior to non-

Christians (outsiders). Christians are not the exclusive brokers of God's grace. The irony is that many Christians claim superiority and monopoly in the name of the Jesus who never claimed anything for himself—and who insisted that his disciples ask nothing for themselves.　2002

We can have it only if we do not possess it. That is the ultimate irony of Jesus' talk about God's realm.　2002

For Jesus, God's domain was immediately and powerfully present, as though he stood with God at creation and with God at the eschaton, and understood the full intermediate ebb and flow of history. When disenchantment set in, following his death, God's domain was pushed off into some future by his followers, first into the immediate future, and then into the distant future, because they had lost the overpowering presence of God. And if God's domain were to come in the future, there would be a delay, and a delay required a second coming of the messiah—of Jesus—to achieve what his first coming had not. In other words, the overwhelming vision of Jesus was translated back into ordinary apocalyptic expectations of that time, expectations that some of Jesus' followers had learned from John the Baptist. The vision of Jesus was thereby domesticated, assimilated to conventional apocalyptic views.　2002

Jesus pointed steadily at the kingdom of God in evidence all around him; his disciples first caught a glimpse of the kingdom but soon began to stare exclusively at the pointing finger.　1997

The fellow who runs the granary down the street in our industrial park frequently plays fetch the ball with his dog. Occasionally he pretends to throw the ball and, when the dog is looking away, actually throws it. Because the dog has not observed the trajectory of the ball, he sits at his master's feet and waits. His master points in the direction of the ball. The dog barks at his pointing finger.

Human beings are like dogs: Jesus points to some horizon, some fabulous yonder, something he called God's domain, which he sees but to which we are blind, and like dogs, we bark at the pointing finger, oblivious to the breathtaking view.　1992

For Jesus the old age was ending, and the new age beginning right there and right then. It is difficult for us to imagine how profoundly this conviction altered the landscape of Jesus' everyday world, how radically it modified his notion of how to behave and think.

The first and most difficult point for us to grasp is that this change had already taken place for him. He did not need to argue for it, he did not cite prophecy that it was to take place, he did not calculate the day or hour when it was to arrive. For him the furniture of the world had been rearranged. He seems never to have doubted that the kingdom of his vision was more real than the deceptive landscape taken for granted by others. God's rule was a fact to which he could only submit.   1993

The kingdom as Jesus sees it breaking in will arrive in disenchanting and disarming form: not as a mighty cedar astride the lofty mountain height but as a lowly garden herb. The kingdom is asserted with comic relief: what it is and what it will do, it will be and do, appearances to the contrary notwithstanding. It will erupt out of the power of weakness and refuse to perpetuate itself by the weakness of power, to translate into Pauline terms (I Cor 1:18–31).   1975

For Jesus, God's domain is as near as the neighbor, as close as someone pounding on your door at midnight asking for a loaf of bread or cup of sugar, as imminent as a beggar with an outstretched hand.   NO DATE

If Jesus were the first Christian, it was not because he had faith in himself—because he confessed himself to be the messiah—but because he had faith in God's reign. Most scholars agreed that Jesus talked about the kingdom of God, not about himself, contrary to the Fourth Gospel. It is thus possible that the first followers of Jesus trusted what Jesus trusted: the rule of God.   1997

Jesus, it is said, came proclaiming the reign of God. The reign to which his words pointed was not accompanied by observable signs. No one could say, "There it is!" or "Over here!" (Luke 17:21).

Those about him, though craning their necks, could not see what he was talking about. Because they could not see it, they were inclined to think the reign to which he pointed was unreal. They did not know and could not guess that they were under the spell of another horizon. However, the poor and the destitute, the tax collectors and prostitutes occasionally saw it, and rejoiced. For them, Jesus' magic was stronger than the magic of habituated sensibility.　1975

The horizon of the reign of God does not parade itself as THE TRUTH.　1975

In God's realm, we are to ask and expect to receive, seek and expect to find, knock in the certainty that a door will be opened. That confidence is expressed in the petition to provide us with bread for the day, a request literally addressed to God but in fact directed to other human beings. Jesus never suggests that manna will fall out of heaven or that some miracle will result in the multiplication of loaves and fish. God's largesse comes by way of the generosity of others. It is the rule in honor/shame societies that hospitality is expected, indeed required, when a request is advanced on behalf of a late traveler. The same can be said of debts—real money debts. One prayer petition asks that our debts be remitted to the extent we have remitted the debts of others. Once again, it is literally a prayer addressed to God, but its fulfillment depends on the actions of human beings who are under obligation to each other. God is not expected to interfere or to rectify an injustice or imbalance. Mortals are expected to achieve that goal for themselves.　2002

The real epic of Israel, of course, is not the story of Saul, David, and Solomon, but the myth of the Exodus. The epic of the Davidic kingdom endorses traditional values: power, wealth, position, authority. The Exodus, on the other hand, is inaugurated by the departure of slaves from Egypt, followed by years of wandering in the Sinai desert. That epic is more appropriate to the parables. But as Christian orthodoxy developed, it adopted the myth of the external redeemer as its epic, as the story which functions as the narrative frame for Jesus of Nazareth. In the myth of the outside redeemer, the hero is supernatural; he or she performs acts beyond the ability of normal human beings. However, in God's domain, as

Jesus depicts it, the lowest of the low have the power to do every-thing for themselves by putting their trust in the Father. To have forgiveness all they need to do is forgive others. They need only ask and they will receive. The parables call for repeated departure from Egyptian slavery and wandering in the desert. The parables thus undermine their own primary referent, God's domain.   2002

Ten Words
of Jesus

*W*hat are the contours of the divine domain as Jesus sees them? I have attempted to summarize them in ten words. I am tempted to call these the new ten words, as the Ten Commandments are called. But they are not commandments and I do not recommend them as a monument for courthouse lobbies.

1. The divine domain belongs to the poor.

In the first beatitude, the poor learn, to their surprise, that the divine domain belongs to them. That contravenes appearances.

2. Love your enemies.

The admonition to love enemies is an invitation to transcend tribal boundaries.

3. Hate your father and mother.

Jesus tells potential followers that they must abandon their primary structures of socialization if they want to be his disciples.

4. Whoever tries to hang on to life will forfeit it, but whoever forfeits life will preserve it.

In the divine domain, according to Jesus, to seek to preserve life is to lose life. To have life we must give it away.

5. Forgive and you'll be forgiven.

This assurance is an oblique rejection of the brokerage system. He advises his followers to function as their own priests.

6. No prophet is welcome on his home turf.

Jesus was an outsider and outcast. He was unwelcome in his hometown, like other prophets.

7. If someone sues you for your coat, give him the shirt off your back to go with it.

In a two-garment society, that would have produced gales of laughter. Humor has a way of undermining the domination structures.

Thus far I have spoken only of the alterations to the human social world. Jesus also has some hints about the cosmic context that differ from the received worldview.

8. According to Jesus, there is no room for demons in the divine domain.

The fall of Satan is the first huge step in sweeping the heavens clear of gods and demons.

9. Consider the lilies and the sparrows.

The divine domain extends even to the flowers and the birds.

10. God sends the rain on both the good and the bad, and causes the sun to shine on both the just and unjust.

The cosmos is indifferent to human projects and goals.   2007

Good
Samaritan

*W*hich of these three proved to be neighbor? It is a question on which we choke, as did Jews of that period. And that is to be our jolt, we who belong to another period: as victims we are "loved" by the enemy, the heretic, the biologically impure, the immoral, the outcast, the nobody. To the southerner, the good Samaritan may be the Negro; to the northerner, the southerner; to the American, the Russian; to the Russian, the American; to the John Bircher, the comsymp; to the liberal, the demagogue; to the modern Jew, the Arab; to the Arab, the Jew; to the Baptist, the Catholic; to the Catholic, the Unitarian. The Good Samaritan is precisely the one whom we do not expect to stop beside us on that road, the one by whom we do not want to be picked up in our battered condition, the one by whom we do not want to be loved.   1964

The Samaritan is the one whom the victim does not, could not expect would help, indeed does not want help from. . . . Every hearer has to hear it in *his* or *her* own way. The future which the parable discloses is the future of every hearer who grasps and is grasped by being in the ditch. . . . The poor traveler is literally the victim of a ruthless robber. So were the poor, the lame, the blind, and the others whom Jesus drew to his side. In fact, one has to understand oneself as the victim in order to be eligible.   1966

The Samaritan does not love with side glances at God. The need of neighbor alone is made self-evident, and the Samaritan responds without other motivation.   1966

The Samaritan discloses in wordless deeds the world in which love as event is indigenous, a world that is made present, to those attending, in the deedful words of the parables.   1966

The Samaritan as parable forces on its hearers the question: who among you will permit himself or herself to be served by a Samaritan? In a general way it can be replied: only those who are unable to refuse. Permission to be served by the Samaritan is thus inability to resist. Put another way, all who are truly victims, truly disinherited, truly helpless, have no choice but to give themselves up to mercy. And mercy comes from the quarter from which it is least expected. Grace is always a surprise. 1982

As a parable, the Samaritan is a very powerful instrument. It sets the message of Jesus in unequivocal terms for its audience. No one could mistake. It explains why IRS officials and prostitutes understand the kingdom, whereas theologians, Bible scholars, and professional pietists do not. It explains why a hated alien must be the instrument of grace. It makes pretense on the part of the listener impossible. No other parable in the Jesus tradition carries a comparable punch. The Christian community moralizes it in order to be able to live with it, and that is inverted testimony to its power. 1982

Once it is understood that the parable of the Samaritan is a fantasy—a fantasy about God's domain, an order of reality that feeds on but ultimately overturns the everyday world—it is but a short step to the view that the story is not about a stickup on Jericho boulevard at all. It is about a new order of things, a new reality that lies beyond, but just barely beyond, the everyday, the humdrum, the habituated. Then the parable is understood as an invitation to cross over. 1996

The man in the ditch on the Jericho road was shocked that a Samaritan would stop to help him on that dangerous stretch (Luke 10:30–35). He resisted assistance because it was contaminating coming from a foreigner. But he was helpless. So the Samaritan put him on his beast, takes him into town, and pays the innkeeper to look after him until he recovers. This exaggerated and humorous protocol drives the point home: under the terms of God's rule, help is available, but it cannot be made subject to conditions. It will always come as a surprise, because it will be undeserved and will come from a source we did not, could not, expect. 1992

Think now of the aphorisms of Jesus and ask yourself which of his sayings goes with this parable. One thinks immediately of "love your enemies." But while the admonition comports with the actions of the Samaritan, it does not pertain to the victim. Remember, the initial perspective of the story, the point of view we were obliged to adopt as our own, was that of the fellow who had been robbed and left for dead. From our point of view, the injunction would have to be turned around: "Let your enemies love you."

In either form, the admonition is unthinkable in a tribal honor/shame culture. Love was reserved for tribal members. Hate was the order of the day for aliens and members of other tribes. The story simply subverts the lived world of the peasants in Jesus' audience. Yet someone, or some few, apparently caught sight of what he was talking about, saw how revolutionary it was, and decided to lay claim to the new world of God's domain in exchange for the old universe of tribal enmity and frustrated hopes.   2002

Scholars are sometimes asked why Jesus was killed. Very complex political, social, and theological answers have been given to this question, any or all of which have some degree of validity. But a simple rejoinder may be quite adequate: The parable of the Samaritan could easily have gotten Jesus killed.   2002

Hard Sayings

L ove your enemies is probably the most radical thing Jesus ever said. Unless, of course, one considers the parable of the Samaritan. There the admonition is to let your enemies love you. 1999

The next most radical aphorism is perhaps the hardest of all the sayings in the Jesus repertoire. "Unless you hate your father and mother, and wife and children and brothers and sisters—yes, even life itself—you're no disciple of mine" (Luke 14:26).

This saying is about breaking the ties that bind. Christians have been inclined to ignore this saying for most of its history, or have remodeled it. Matthew has simply turned the saying around to make it more acceptable to polite society: If you love your father and mother more than me . . . you are not worthy of me" (Matt 10:37). His community did not like, or did not understand, the radical demand in its original form.

Jesus was probably thinking of an extended family, perhaps of three or four or five generations, living in a one or two room house, presided over by an aging patriarch who made life and death decisions for everyone in the family. Under such circumstances, he might well have indicated that his followers must break their ties with the family enclave in order to be open to the radically new way of relating to God's domain. That makes eminent sense. Especially if we do not insist that he meant "hate" literally.

The contrast between the love of enemies and the hatred of families is striking. The one blows away the tribal boundary, the other demolishes family ties. Kinship in the kingdom means dwelling in a house without walls. 1999

Somewhere near the heart of Jesus' vision is this simple admonition that from the very first has inspired and troubled his followers; love your enemies. 2002

> God causes the sun to rise on both the bad and the good,
> and sends rain on both the just and the unjust.
>
> —Matthew 5:45b

That's the basis of a fairly radical notion of God. A God who treats all human beings evenhandedly is not in much evidence in either testament. The God pictured in the Bible is highly partial and often quite vindictive. The God of Jesus, in contrast, appears to have no favorites. The cosmic background of life is apparently neutral and therefore inclusive.   2002

Jesus' vision of the domain of God is counterintuitive. The divine domain runs counter to recipe knowledge.   2002

Jesus of the Gospels, Creedal Christ

*J*esus of Nazareth contributed very little to the development of what emerged as orthodox Christianity. 2003

For the Gnostics, Jesus is a heavenly teacher who instructs his disciples from his exalted state. The New Testament gospels, in contrast, represent Jesus as a sage prior to his death; however, they also make Jesus talk like a Christian. 1995

Jesus' admirers turned Jesus the iconoclast into Jesus the icon. They exchanged his view of God's domain for their vision of him. 2002

The proclamation of the first missionaries (the Greek term for it is kerygma) and the derivative creed may not be entirely appropriate for the gospel of Jesus. The kerygma and creed are preoccupied with the status of Jesus rather than with God's domain; with the king rather than the kingdom; with an icon rather than the iconoclast. The members of the early Jesus movement were preoccupied with the status of the apostles and themselves, rather than with Jesus' vision of a boundaryless, brokerless community. The evidence is that they created a creed with an empty center: There is very little left of the Jesus of the parables and aphorisms in that creed. 2002

The creedal Christ, no less than the best scholarly reconstructions of Jesus, is an idol that invites shattering. Both must "yield to the facts, which . . . are sometimes the most radical critics of all," as Schweitzer put it. 1996

Christianity as we know it did not originate with Jesus of Nazareth. Jesus was not the first Christian. 1996

In the transmission of the Jesus tradition several things transpire simultaneously:

1. The tension in the language of Jesus is released.

2. The terms of that language are assimilated to previously habituated categories so that Jesus is made to compete within a pregiven life-world.

3. Jesus is painted into the narrative picture as the certifier of the new reality.

4. God is made immanent to the process.

5. These developments lead to the disenchantment of the fantasy, so that the arrival of the kingdom is pushed off into the future.

6. The Messiah must then return to achieve what he did not achieve the first time through.   1989

Contemporary
Culture

*W*e need a rebirth of the Liberal Spirit. We require a neo-liberalism with fresh intellectual rigor, immaculate honesty, and moral muscle, circumspectly informed by the sciences and awash in toe-tapping cadences inspired by the need to sing and dance. The new spirit will wither if not allied with the arts.   2007

The art of conversation is declining in our culture. In some quarters the death-rattle is audible. Even scholars, of all people, too rarely give themselves to the luxury of an unhurried conversation, the type of discourse in which participants listen as well as speak. We talk to each other a great deal, but we do not hear what is said in return. Indeed, we frequently do not even pay attention to what we ourselves are saying. It is as though conversants were mouths without ears, yapping away simultaneously in the midst of unattended bedlam. And we tend to write, to process words, in the same unreflective mode: we crank out paragraphs and essays that are no more than occasions to manhandle some subject or browbeat readers.   1975

In the modern industrialized West we have been in transition for at least 500 years, ever since Copernicus transformed our notions of the solar system. It has been extremely difficult for some to adjust to the idea that the earth is a heavenly body rather than a lid for the fires of hell below. Francis Bacon and Isaac Newton laid down the blueprint for the scientific revolution and the new historicism. A work ethic replaced monastic asceticism and gave rise to a middle class, the foundation of all modern democracies. Endless religious wars produced the secular state, which some still regard as anathema to religion, but which in fact is protection against the office of Holy Inquisition. Reason, observation, experiment—the trinity of the Enlightenment—sponsored learning and freedom of inquiry. As late as the 1960s most of us experienced a fresh assault on the conceptual and moral certainties we had inherited which amounted almost to a second enlightenment. Many of the conflicts in our present society stem from that single decade.

Then, without warning, on 11 September 2001 the Global Age arrived.   2005

Insecurity and uncertainty have produced a plethora of political bullies: fundamentalists on the right and politically correct liberals on the left insist that we all adopt their points of view. I don't like bullies, big or little, human or divine, smart or dumb. I prefer to make up my own mind after careful review.   1996

Straightjackets of opinion are as restrictive among liberals as they are among fundamentalists.   1996

The pursuit of the "real" is prompted by the conviction that what is really real is not what is commonly taken to be real. The quest of the real is thus grounded in the circumspection that the "world" of John and Jane Doe is phony, a cardboard stage on which they act out pre-assigned roles in the common comedy, the script for which the received tradition has already been fixed. The center of gravity in the literature and art of our time is that the received "world" is a grand farce, a make-believe construction saturated with illusion from top to bottom. Henry Miller expresses this conviction poignantly by asserting that those who inhabit the continent are sound asleep and dreaming a grand nightmare.   1975

Not to recognize this truth—that human beings are in part their own creators—is a deception of the most fundamental order.   1975

The physical sciences and preoccupation with the literal have nearly killed the imagination. That does not mean that I want to give up my refrigerator and modern medicine, both of which owe their efficacy to the sciences. But it does mean that refrigeration and surgery do not cover all the needs of the mind and spirit. There are some things that cooling and lancing will not cure. The ability to perceive the nonliteral dimensions of our world is the victim of our inclination to exchange a refreshed sense of the world for a mess of technical pottage.   1996

I am not among those who think the Enlightenment was a bad thing. The Enlightenment brought us tolerance for alien forms of faith, created the secular state to referee the conflicts between warring religious factions, established the priesthood of all believers, and created a middle class with a powerful work ethic that is the foundation of all modern democracies. And the Enlightenment made the empirical sciences possible by discrediting the church as a reality authority.   2003

National and World Affairs

*T*errorism and precipitous responses to it almost always produce the opposite of what is intended.   2001

The obvious truth on which we might build our long-range response and policy is this: "You can't build your security on someone else's insecurity."   2001

It is time for ordinary Americans to unite, to take back their political parties, and to demand better than we are offered. We have a right to real leadership. We perhaps do not deserve better, given our penchant for the easy solution, for the special-interest-serving political hack. Yet our short-sighted and mindless behavior has been learned from bankrupt local, state, and national leaders of the last forty years. We can afford to be children no more. Our dreams will be gone if we do not awake from our deep national sleep.   1992

We want to place at the helm of our nation those who will put the long-term future above petty politics and quick fixes; we want as leaders those who will not pander to myriads of special interests; we want durable policies that will bring us slowly but surely to the level of national and regional self-respect and self-restraint necessary to our continuing prosperity as a people. Above all, we want as leaders those who serve all the people, not just a select few.   1992

Americans must be awakened to a new stewardship of the land, water, and air. Prosperity is not prosperity if life has to be lived in a sewer. There is no good economic reason profit and prosperity cannot be linked with the proper regard for the environment. Indeed, cleaning up and preserving our human habitat is the only way to a prosperous future. Those who claim these two goals are inimical to each other are fools and should be shunned. All that is lacking is the will to join them together. 1992

If private citizens followed the example of the government, we would all be in the poorhouse for there would be nothing to tax. 1992

The FBI insisted that all it asked of David Koresh and the Branch Davidians was that they surrender to "duly constituted authority." Koresh and his followers, like other recent cult leaders and disciples, had already surrendered to what they took to be the one and only "duly constituted authority," God. Neither the FBI nor the ATS gave the slightest hint, in fifty-one days of the Texas siege, that they understood the competing claims involved in this stand-off. The emperor and God were again at war. 1993

The United States should insist that Israel and the Palestinians resolve their differences and do so equitably and promptly. Unless the American Jewish community supports this demand, it will be difficult for the U.S. to succeed in imposing its will on the two parties. A half-century is enough time to have worked out the issues that divide the two. It is time for healing to begin. The conflict over Palestine is not warranted by the ancient faith of either the Israelis or the Muslims. We now know that those scriptural claims on the part of all parties, Christian included, are fictitious and no basis for political resolution. 2001

I am filled with a sense of foreboding. . . . The literacy levels in matters both religious and scientific has fallen to a dangerous low. The introduction of religion into politics may inspire new religious wars sponsored by the state. In a democracy, people cannot be both ignorant and free, as Thomas Jefferson once said. Moreover, the institutions we might have expected to assist with the transition from the old symbols and myths to new ones are either unprepared or are unwilling to do so; rather, they are beleaguered and defensive.

I am saddened that many of our colleagues in colleges and universities have elected to sit out the struggle in the comfort of their carrels. Beyond these matters, I am alarmed at the prospect of having to negotiate new shoals as globalization increases. The explosion of the world's population and the confrontation between the world's faith traditions means that political, economic, and social problems may overwhelm us.   2003

We have been in the global age since 9/11. Or at least it has finally dawned on us Americans since then that we do live in one world.   2002

American
Religious Life

*T*he parochialism of the churches is undoubtedly the product of an entrenched bureaucracy rather than the deep conviction of the average member. 2002

In the United States, the common view is that on the subject of religion one opinion is as good as another. That view is a recipe for chaos and that is just about what we have in reporting religion. The media frequently prefer to encourage chaos by trafficking in the sensational, the marginal, the trite, on which they enlarge by sponsoring confrontations between opinionated but uninformed parties. 2002

The Christian right has come to power in a vacuum of information. 2001

Fundamentalism is actually an acute form of secularism, one that blinks its own circumscribed knowledge of the tradition, in short, its own ignorance, in the name of piety, and arrogantly announces its utopian and antiseptic schemes as a grand confidence game for the spiritually destitute. 1986

Fundamentalisms of various types are efforts to turn back the clock to the sixteenth century, to the infancy of the Enlightenment, to the clear and distinct idea, much as the Essenes attempted to reverse time in Jesus' day by moving out to the desert and establishing isolated, insulated, uncontaminated enclaves. 1996

There is very little ideologically that separates the fundamentalists in the U.S. from the Islamic and Israeli fundamentalists elsewhere. The difference is that American fundamentalists have not gotten control of the government. The current effort to breach the wall that separates church and state will bring us to grief if allowed to proceed. 2001

We should encourage the Muslims to develop an openly critical relation to their own traditions. It is no longer acceptable for Muslims to insist that the Hebrew bible and the New Testament contain substantial errors, while the Qur'an is infallible. The contract issued on Salman Rushdie is a silent reminder that Islam is not ready for a critical exchange with Jewish and Christian scholars. But then neither are Robertson and Falwell. 2001

Churchgoers have a Sunday morning experience followed by a Monday morning reality check. 2003

Many Christian folk are hanging onto their Sunday morning experience by their fingertips, hoping for reprieve. Or, they have abandoned the institutional church altogether. They find themselves in this plight because the gospel and its institutional trappings are no longer plausible within the emerging new paramount reality. If we do not modify church practice, the Sunday morning experience will sink finally into irrelevance and oblivion. We stand at the crossroads. 2003

American pastor-directors no longer regard themselves primarily as the servants of the Word but as builders of congregational morale and promoters of the common culture. Unless it can be construed as group counseling, hermeneutics will not have much bite for them. Pretty much the same can be said of their ecclesiastical superiors.

[M]any American theologians and churchmen, unhappy with the denominational ethos and smarting under the increasing alienation of the religious ghetto from authentically secular culture, have gone outside the church in order to enter into dialogue with the secular world—the arts in particular. 1964

The poet, it is often said, has replaced the priest. The priest has become the mediator of dead words and an inert messiah; the poet seeks to mediate living language and thus a risen Christ. Whether the poet ought to come off so handsomely is a moot point, but the church and its priestly hierarchy have been unequivocally indicted. 1968

Jesus Christ Superstar and Superman have displaced the savior of the traditional Christian creed, the Jesus of the early confessions and the gospels, indeed, all the forms of the messiah figure known to us, Jewish and well as Christian. Cinematic saviors, on the screen and in the White House, have taken top billing in the American epic, without serious reference or accommodation to the portrait that reaches across the centuries to us out of the gospels. 1986

Religious traditions and mythologies have not been forsaken in America: they have merely been profaned. 1986

The synagogue is the alleged custodian of the Hebrew epic, the church of the Christian story. And yet these institutions have all but abrogated their historic roles as troubadours of the tradition. 1986

The epic of the Exodus and the crossing of the Jordan into the Promised Land was better understood by Martin Luther King than by Jim Jones. King knew that black Americans could only reach the far shore by continually crossing over, repeatedly and painfully; Jim Jones thought that the promised land was a place on some map, like Disneyland, to which one could readily move, were one so inclined. 1986

Truth to tell, Cardinal Ratzinger and the TV evangelists represent the worst of the Inquisition and totalitarian religion. 1989

During a recent pastors' school in the Northwest, a colleague of mine asked the pastors, at my suggestion, to find out from their parishioners what stories they lived by. He asked them specifically to take a survey to discover whether any part of the biblical story was still alive as myth, and if so, what part. In the weeks to follow, the reports he received were nothing short of astonishing.

As it turns out, Protestants in the Northwest do have a living biblical myth, and that story is the epic of the exodus and the settlement in Canaan. And, what is more, they associate that story with their own frequent excursions into the wilderness on weekends and holidays: they believe themselves the better for living on the edge of a wilderness, a frontier, and they think that accounts, in large part, for their piety. Moreover, they think God commissioned Americans to come to this continent and found a new society, a city set on a hill for all to see and imitate. But these same protestant parishioners do not have a Christian story, that is, they have no story of which Jesus is a part. Their story is essentially the Hebrew epic.

Americans live on the terrain of these mythic spaces. Their politics, their perceptions of themselves, and their lifestyles are conditioned by them. And the categories they have chosen in relation to which they understand themselves are biblical. That should give pause to those of us who toil in the pages of the Hebrew and Christian scriptures. And it should suggest to us that our work may indeed be relevant—crucially relevant to life in this hemisphere. For that reason it is time we came out of our windowless studies and opened up shop in the marketplace.   1990

I discovered that by and large what my students learned in seminary did not get passed on to parish members; in fact, it seems to have little or no bearing on the practice of ministry at all.   1996

The claims made by Jerry Falwell and Pat Robertson about the bible and the Christian point of view are a contradiction of everything scholars know about these matters. It is a clear dereliction of duty on the part of those scholars to remain silent in the face of such a challenge.   1992

I accept Jesus as *my personal savior.* Personal savior means, for many if not most, Jesus as I personally perceive him.   1992

The appeal of the individualized Jesus is to the notion, firmly rooted in the American mind, that religion is a private affair. The typical Americana insists: "What I think about religion is none of your business." Moreover, the separation of church and state has been taken to mean the right to remain ignorant. Americans have exercised both rights to their fullest: Ignorance combined with privatization has resulted, for the most part, in the distortion of Jesus in the interest of causes to which he would probably have been opposed, or has produced a popular, saccharin, antiseptic, teddy-bear Jesus. And both church and synagogue have been content to allow these images of Jesus to be promoted and exploited by televangelists and purveyors of pulp religious literature.   1992

The clergy have been caught in the tension between the churches they have taken oaths to serve and the scholars who were their mentors in seminaries. Like other rational human beings, some have opted for the safe course, which is not to offend patrons of the parish in order to protect their pensions. This intellectual sacrifice has made them theological eunuchs in the temple of the Lord. Others have given up and quit the service of the church altogether. Still others—a few—have dared to broach the fundamental issues and behave like prophets, at great expense to themselves. A handful told the truth as they knew it from the start.   1999

The mainline churches face a fundamental crisis of faith: in a preemptory way they have suppressed the questions people are asking, or would ask if empowered to do so, and so have left themselves and their parishioners vulnerable. Church bureaucrats too often admonish, "Don't rock the boat," or they urge us not to injure the good work the church is doing in other domains by posing embarrassing questions. Worst of all, they ask us not to disturb the faith of simple believers, as though the suppression of knowledge can somehow advance the faith. In so doing, they are postponing a rendezvous with the issues that are emptying the churches and crippling the intellectual integrity of the Christian tradition.   1996

Americans consider religion entirely a private affair. For most, in matters religious one opinion is deemed to be as good as another. In the university lecture hall, the professor of theoretical physics or biochemistry is seldom contradicted by the heady student; the distinguished scholar of classics or the teacher of Chinese rarely faces students who think they know better; but instructors in religion are repeatedly confronted by untutored sophomores who demand equal time and disproportionate attention for their ill-conceived certitudes. They do so usually on the basis of something they have learned from crusaders on campus sponsored by fundamentalist promoters. Knowledge appears to make no contribution to the credentials of an authority; opinions firmly held, expressed loudly, and buttressed by ignorance are quite adequate.   1996

During the half century that separates us from World War II, we have come to the end of the Christian era. By that I do not mean that Christianity has come to an end; I mean rather that the hegemony of the Christianized, industrialized West over the rest of the globe has come to an end. We are passing through a radical cultural transition which marks the close of the Christian era and the beginning of a global society.   2000

With his telescope, Galileo changed our perceptions of space and time forever; Einstein and Hubble only made matters worse. However, the churches continue to pretend that nothing really has changed with respect to the mythic framework of the gospel. The old world is gone, and all the church's horses and all the church's men cannot put that world together again.   2000

Most churchgoers have no need for us [biblical scholars] because we produce a less than robust Jesus who is of no interest to thriving congregations.   1989

Confessions, like prayer, can be the most deceptive cover-ups of all our pious practices.   1996

The pulpit has become the locus of the soft assurance rather than the source of hard information. Parish ministers wither and die on a vine that is neither pruned nor watered—unless they take matters into their own hands. The least common denominator and the collection plate have taken over Christian education. Worse yet, the spiritual and intellectual leaders of Christian communities have allowed uninformed parishioners to determine the content of the gospel. In a television interview, a Lutheran pastor insisted that his parishioners would go down the street to a church that taught fundamentalism, if he did not teach it. That does not strike me as a particularly prophetic response to the requirements of the gospel. I wonder what happened to his moral integrity.　1966

I started out to be a parish minister but soon learned that passion for truth was not compatible with that role. In self-defense I became a scholar.　1966

Churches no longer know what their mission is. They are content to endorse the United Way and drift.　1996

Ethics

*T*he Big Bang does not accord humankind a privileged place in the scheme of things. Moreover, our record as custodians of the biosphere we inhabit has not done much to commend us as superior life forms.   2003

The task we now face is monumental: we must convince ourselves and the rest of humanity that the earth is not ours to plunder.   2003

We need to feel at home in the universe without parental assurances that we can have the order without the chaos. Since God won't do it, we need to take the responsibility for ourselves, for each other, for truth, and for the planet.   2003

Jesus advocates love of the enemy, which means that God's domain transcends the tribe, the ethnic groups, and the nation.   2003

The chief test of the authentic quest for truth in our time is not ideological but ethical. It is not what we believe that is crucial but what we do. In some circles, joining a church means accepting an ideology; it should mean caring for one's neighbor. When ideology dominates, the ethical light dims.   1966

It is a source of constant bewilderment and frustration that Jesus had so little to say by way of explicit direction for getting on in the world. He did of course leave perfectly lucid injunctions like "love your enemies," and "give to everyone who begs of you." But anyone who has trudged, automatic weapon slung over the shoulder, through the jungle of some guerilla war, or walked the streets of a major city, knows how unrealistic these maxims are. Some of

Jesus' teachings are comfortable because they no longer apply or are thought not to apply; still others the early church qualified or simply inverted, as the means of making them useful. It is astonishing how few of Jesus' words, in their original form, are suitable as a base for prudential moral reasoning. 1975

The conversation of Jesus with the rich young ruler (Luke 18:18ff) is usually taken to turn on the question of the responsible stewardship of possessions. Yet Jesus demands that the rich man, in addition to observing the commandments, sell all that he has and distribute the proceeds to the poor. The moral dilemma in which that places the rich, the powerful, even the church, when understood literally, is excruciating. The moral dilemma is painful even when understood properly as a metaphor: Jesus invited then and the power of his language invites now to set things free, to enjoy them without possessing, to embrace without acquiring. It would be an exhilarating but perilous adventure. 1975

Ambiguity is a tool Jesus employs to shift the responsibility for decision and action to his listeners, and thus avoid prescribing behavior for his followers. 2002

We have come late to the realization that our well being depends on the well being of all life forms in the biosphere. The loss of the ozone, the pollution of lakes and rivers, the wanton destruction of rain forests, the insatiable need for oil from the ground and fish from the sea, are robbing us of any tenable future. We needn't wait for the big crunch a few billion years hence to end it all; we are creating the big crunch for ourselves here and now. 2007

Christianity at its heart is not moralistic. In its finest hours it is ethical. At its worst it is creedal—creeds are designed to exclude and expunge rather than include and nourish. 1996

The task we now face is monumental: we must convince ourselves and the rest of humanity that the earth is not ours to plunder. 2003

Trust

*T*he word we formerly used for trust was faith. But faith has been spoiled by its popular connotations. It has come to mean intellectual assent to the standard doctrines of one's religious tradition. When even more narrowly defined, faith means believing in believing. It is then regarded as a supernatural virtue that enables one to believe that God has revealed the divine will through Christ and the church. So we have come to speak of "faith traditions," which represent the compendia of convictions that characterizes particular religious communities.

Trust does not involve believing something or in something. Trust involves seeing the world and other people for what they are when viewed through God's eyes. Trust means acting on that perception. That is the heart of Jesus' vision.

Suppose you trust the view that the world is flat. Would you board a ship to sail around the world? Would you book a flight on an airplane that purports to take you to the other side of the globe? Or, to change the illustration, if you were not convinced that a medium could predict your future, would you pay her for advice? Trust means willingness to act on what you take to be ultimately true.   2002

As an itinerant, Jesus apparently trusted God absolutely. Trust in God translates in practice as trust in neighbor, in those one meets on the road, in the laws of hospitality. . . . Celebration is the by-product of that trust. In other words, celebration is the endorsement of trust. Celebration nourishes trust. Celebration is the heart of liturgy in God's domain.   2002

Most of us in Western industrialized societies are immersed in a work ethic: we labor to produce the goods of life and the good life and believe our virtue resides in that labor. On the other hand, Jesus advocated a trust ethic.   1999

Celebration is the by-product of trust. It is also the joy attendant upon not being left out.   1999

The complement of trust is integrity. The one leads inevitably to the other. We cannot trust and dissemble simultaneously. We owe it to ourselves and to our friends to be up front about where we are and how we got there.   1999

Francis of Assisi was hoeing in his garden one day. Someone asked him what he would do if he knew the world were going to end the next day. He paused and then responded: "Hoe in my garden."   1992

Jesus advises those around him not to fret about food and cloth-ing. His Father looks after the sparrow, he says, and they are a dime a dozen. With typical hyperbole, he insists that God counts the hairs on human heads. Perhaps that is the reason Jesus takes no thought for shelter—he has no place to lay his head, unlike the foxes and birds. Without permanent address and unemployed, he was a vagabond king.   1993

How does one get into God's Kingdom? Jesus insisted that people can only enter the kingdom if they don't deserve to. These undeserving, like the prodigal and the petty tax official, are like the homeless in rags who find themselves unexpectedly at a White House dinner party.

Strictly speaking, however, arrival in the kingdom is not even possible. Arrival is by departure only. Entrance into God's domain is the same thing as exodus; it is the quest of Abraham for a new ancestral home. Permission to pass is not required; trust is the key that unlocks the door.   1993

In God's domain, everyone must trust for himself or herself. There is no such thing as vicarious trust. The existentialists used to put the point well by saying that no one can take a bath for you. In God's domain, nobody can have your trust for you. There are no surrogates. There are no external redeemers. Thus the orthodox Christian epic is a corruption of the plot of the parable. However,

the cross is an appropriate symbol for the Christian mode of
existence, if by the cross we understand that we are all pilgrims
embarked on an exodus that is under girded by nothing other than
trust.   2002

Forgiveness

*I*n a garden variety society, bad behavior is punished, sometimes severely, and good behavior rewarded, sometimes generously. At the extremes lie heaven and hell.

Jesus, on the other hand, was not impressed with the standard schedule of rewards and punishments. In fact, Jesus did not accuse or judge those who knew themselves to be sinners. However, he was scathing in his criticism of the self-righteous and hypocritical. In this, as in other matters, he reverses normal expectations.

He makes forgiveness reciprocal: "Forgive and you'll be forgiven," he says (Luke 6:37). One cannot be a recipient of forgiveness unless or until one is an agent of forgiveness. It's as simple and as difficult as that.   1993

Sometimes when people tell me that I'm on my way to hell because of what I'm doing to the gospels, I say to them, "But, of course, you'll forgive me, since your forgiveness depends on it."   1994

Jesus took the right of forgiveness out of the hands of God and priest and reassigned it exclusively to those who needed it: to be forgiven all one need do is forgive.   1996

Bible

*T*he biblical corpus is large enough to warrant, even require, selective attention. And because it has suffered overatten-tion, its language has been overlaid with tons of obfuscating debris. To change the metaphor, few literary compendia in the Western tradition have been so completely rinsed of resonances by the waters of endless repetition and uncritical interpretation. Is it possible to restore some of those resonances or cart away some of that debris? 1975

The Bible . . . provides us with a paradox: to take the biblical text, as fixed in language, as inspired, is to resist the respeaking and rehearing of the word. Yet, respeaking and rehearing must be in continuity with the original speaking and hearing. How is it possible to keep the word living and true at the same time? 1975

The interpreter who seeks to determine not merely the meaning of the Bible but also the truth of the Bible, will almost inevitably test his or her interpretation by reference to what he or she, the inter-preter, takes to be true, and thus finally by reference to his or her own opinions and convictions. By thus forcing the truth question upon the text, he or she is treating the bible with "gross irrever-ence" by making it echo his own convictions. The only way to steer clear of this fallacy and so honor the text is to confine interpretation to its legitimate descriptive limit. 1976

The interpretation of scripture from faith to faith . . . runs the danger of circling harmlessly in antiseptic precincts. 1977

Unlike Jesus and Paul, we do not know what it means *not* to presuppose faith, but it will be therapeutic to learn. 1977

The New Testament did not exist as a physical book until the sixteenth century. When it did appear, it was the product of publishers, not of the church.   2000

To listen to what the gospels actually say for their own time and place, as opposed to what we would like them to say, means that individuals must acquire some knowledge of how and when that text was composed and what it meant to its original authors and readers. Bible study often means no more than mining this collection of books composed over more than a millennium for incidental sentences, phrases, images, and schemes that we can employ to indulge our own system of prejudices and preferences. All too often Bible study is a case of the blind congratulating the blind.   1996

The King James Version lulls the reader to sleep; although beautiful, the language is archaic, and the meaning is ensconced in sonorous cadences and Shakespearian phrasing. . . . When Jesus once again becomes a stranger to the modern temper, he will be able to command a fresh hearing.   1996

Religious Literacy

*D*avid Koresh was not well informed about the Bible he evidently worshiped, and had developed an eccentric interpretation of the book of Revelation he so devoutly admired. But then he had been encouraged in his narrow views by other Seventh Day Adventists, Jehovah's Witnesses, Pat Robertson, Jimmy Swaggart, and countless other sects, cults, and evangelists who rail against biblical scholarship while hawking their privileged and private knowledge of the future. The price of religious illiteracy, of the absence of a community of learning and shared judgments, about the Bible is extremely high, as we learned from the Waco holocaust. 1993

In our time, religious literacy has reached a new low in spite of our scholarship, in spite of the remarkable advances in research and publication our academic disciplines have made. 1996

Too many Americans have understood the separation of church and state as the right to remain ignorant about matters religious. It is ironic that so many who believe the Bible is the inerrant word of God cannot name the four canonical gospels, much less the dozen or more extracanonical gospels that once circulated among believers before the age of Constantine (died 337 CE).

Many of these same folk cannot identify the original language of the gospels and cannot specify the century in which the printing press was invented—prior to which no two copies of the gospels were identical because [they were] handmade. Many sincere believers think that Christ is Jesus' family name rather than a title. 1993

Ignorance breeds bigotry. Bigotry opposes the free dissemination and discussion of information and ideas. Newspaper and book burning is the badge of barbarians.

The end of the Christian era is marked . . . by the decline of religious literacy. Religious literacy in American society has degenerated steadily in this century until knowledge of the basic components of the Christian tradition has reached an appalling low. The churches have all but abandoned their traditional role in education. The mainline churches have by and large adopted a defensive posture: they have raised the drawbridge and manned the battlements against women and gays, and against critical knowledge of Christian origins. The enemy turns out to be their own insecurities. 1999

Jesus helped people to see the world in a radically new way. We may not aspire to so much, but we can still think of literacy and learning as extensions of the role of Jesus as sage. 1999

Biblical literacy often creates a crisis of faith. 1999

Apocalypticism

*T*he popular Christian tradition has never been able to resist the temptation to look for signs and portents that herald the presence of the messiah or the arrival of the kingdom. Apocalypticism too soon succumbs to the temptation to assemble a list of supernatural markers.   2002

Few in our society know that Martin Luther, John Calvin, and John Wesley were all uneasy about the place of the book of Revelation in the New Testament. Countless theologians and scholars before and since have had similar misgivings. Revelation, like other apocalypses of its type, is open to interpretive abuse.   1993

We know that the Book of Revelation was never included in the ancient lectionary cycle.   2000

[The Book of] Revelation represents a domestication of everything Jesus stood for.   1992

The surface of the earth is curved to make it impossible to see too far ahead. In all forms of apocalyptic literature, predictions about the future are a riddle—it is as though we are not to know in detail what the future will bring.   1992

Those who claim to be able to predict the end of the world are charlatans and fools. They are playing on ignorance, fear, and gullibility. They should be ignored.   1992

The view that Jesus expected the world to end momentarily, made popular by Albert Schweitzer nearly a century ago, has died a scholarly death.   1992

The apocalyptic visions that constitute the bulk of Revelation do not require Jesus as a central figure. . . . However, in the current popular interpretation of apocalyptic, beliefs about Jesus are made the touchstone of survival.   1992

The apocalyptic hope, then as now, was a popular hope. Jesus took a minority view in rejecting it, but his own view was over-powered by early Christian apocalyptic fervor, which his disciples may have inherited from John the Baptist and other radical groups in the Jordan valley.   1992

When Jesus advises, "No one knows the exact day or minute; no one knows, not even heaven's messengers, not even the son, no one, except the Father" (Mark 13:32), we cannot abide his refusal. We demand to know. We will know. We will twist and torture ancient texts until we come up with the answer Jesus himself refuses to give. For not to know humiliates. Human pride is at stake. Another name for that is human hubris—the demand to have a peer rela-tionship with God. Adam and Eve were ejected from the Garden because divine silence was not good enough for them.   1975

The apocalyptic tradition is relentlessly literal and humorless. It is difficult to crack a joke if you think the world is about to end. And, of course, having a celebration just before Armageddon seems inappropriate.   1999

Biblical Scholars, Biblical Scholarship

*S*cholars of the gospels, most of whom have been trained as textual critics and historians, are frequently tone-deaf. 1996

Scholars have a taste for the expensive, the exotic, and the boring. Their papers must be printed letterpress on the most exquisite paper, however trite the content. They would rather publish two words in Arabic script than 10,000 in basic English. In journal covers, format, and design, they have an unerring eye for the deadly dull. The canonical status of the manual of style is roughly analogous to that of the Koran among Moslems. And these same scholars tend to confuse their tastes with the quality of scholarship. 1971

Because the question of Scripture is just below the surface in American liberal scholarship, it is systematically suppressed in discussion. It is for this reason that the hermeneutical problem cannot be pursued directly. Philological detail and certain ancillary disciplines, such as biblical archaeology, support scholarly "objectivity," while permitting one to evade the question of meaning. The scholar can present an evening of stereopticon slides on biblical sites without so much as touching on the question of religion. Yet, for those with memories of the tradition, viewing the very ground on which the prophets and Jesus walked can kindle a warm glow. It is a question of whether biblical scholarship can continue to trade on a sentiment it is not willing to recognize. 1976

I am proposing that we conduct our work [as biblical scholars] in full public view. If we are to survive as scholars of the humanities, as well as theologians, we must quit the academic closet. And we must begin to sell a product that has some utilitarian value to someone—or which at least appears to have utilitarian value to someone. 1985

It is clear that academicians do not enjoy a positive public image. Let *Time* sum it up: Biblical scholars inhabit the liberal, elite, rarefied halls of academe; we spout ideas and theories that have always been labeled unorthodox and heretical. We are hopelessly divided, wrong-minded in our approach, and basically anti-Semitic in the bargain. We have settled very little; most church-goers have no need for us because we produce a less than robust Jesus who is of no interest to thriving congregations.   1989

Where have all the university students gone? Apparently out into the dark night of consumerism, professional sports, and mindless television. There is no institution to fan that spark, to nourish that tiny thirst for knowledge we so painstakingly implanted in them. Our graduates are isolated, embarrassed to confess their interest in religion, and at a loss to know where to turn for comradeship in the intellectual pursuit of religious knowledge. They can't find good books on the subject, in part because we haven't written for them, in part because booksellers, at the behest of wholesalers, stock mostly trash in the religion section. In the void, they turn in other directions.   1990

Our scholarship in the biblical field is pompously, pathetically, pointlessly fragmented, fractured, frustrated, mostly on trivial matters and for superficial reasons. We are cannibals by preference, it seems. We are oral sadists. This tendency, borne of the resolve to let no untested assertion pass, results in the determination to let no proximate colleague surpass. The professional put down is taken and mistaken for an academic mark up. This needless academic divisiveness hurts us all, without discrimination, including those who indulge in it.   1989

It is profoundly misleading not to give the public an account of the foundations of our learned edifice.   1989

We deliberately put our work beyond reach, for to put it within reach, is to put it in the hands of those who profane and demean it. Populist anti-intellectualism generates academic contempt for the unwashed.   1989

Our concentration on the technical article and monograph is causing the bookstores and the churches to foreclose on us. Even our place in the library, other than the great research libraries, is under threat. If you don't believe me, ask any academic sales rep. 1989

One of the powerful reasons we appear divided as a scholarly guild is that the reference base out of which we all work was laid down largely in the nineteenth and early twentieth centuries. The categories in which those works were cast are seriously out of date. They were also molded on another continent, for quite different issues. We must replace that reference substructure if we are to find our own voice for our own questions. Asking who controls the reference system determines the questions that can be asked next. 1989

Insulated and isolated in the university, rebuffed by the church, and scorned by the public, we have retreated into our academic towers and pretend that what we know is beyond the ken of average mortals. Scholarship in religion, especially in the biblical field, is all but bankrupt. 1996

Biblical criticism has developed a splendid isolation from the other theological disciplines. 1964

Rightly dividing the word of truth is wonderful therapy. 1999

The church bureaucracy and scholarship beholden to the church obediently prefer order to the chaos produced by the spirit.

The preferences of biblical scholarship for order and control are evident in the way its agenda has unfolded in its modern history. A recital of developments will reveal how scholars have moved from the uncontrollable to the staid, steady, and safe. First, form criticism was designed to go behind the written gospels to recover the Jesus tradition in its fluid, wild state. Form criticism came under fire as the subversion of what stands written. We were admonished by the pedants to study the gospels and letters as they appear in our reconstructed Greek texts and not, in some prior hypothetical oral state. Then came redaction criticism with its penchant for ignoring the underlying soul of the tradition and its call to concentrate on how the individual evangelists interpreted Jesus and Paul. Under its tutelage, Mark, Matthew, and Luke displaced Jesus as the source of the primary vision. Finally, reader response criticism reared its egalitarian head to produce the final flattening: Jesus and Paul mean whatever readers take them to mean; as reader, I am the final authority of what they meant.   2000

Methodology is not an indifferent net; it catches only what it is designed to catch.   1975

We can no longer get away with defining events as eschatological or supernatural in order to exempt them from critical review. And we can no longer claim that certain formulations and documents have been endorsed by the holy spirit and so are free of error. We have been trading in those rhetorical devices until our credibility has run out.

Some have insisted, for example, that the virginal conception of Jesus is a "theological" assertion not subject to historical review. Some scholars have begged off investigating the resurrection narratives because they report an "eschatological event," implying a unique event that has no analogies. Still other scholars go right on claiming healing and nature miracles for Jesus as evidence for his divinity while pointedly failing to mention reports of the wondrous deeds of Jesus' contemporaries or dismissing them as inferior examples. In the theological world these tactics come under the heading of apologetics; in the entertainment world they are known as "special effects."   1997

The strength and vitality of any tradition can be measured by the depth and integrity of its continuous self-criticism.   1996

How the scholarly investigation of the gospels affects Christian convictions cannot be the immediate concern of this study or of the work of the Jesus Seminar. Our allegiance is to history—to the historical data we collect and to their interpretation—and not to particular religious interests, not to the Apostles' Creed or the

Westminster Confession of Faith. Whether liberating or not, historical knowledge is the best check we have on the human capacity to deceive ourselves. We are all prone to believe what we want to believe. It is not an act of faith to take the Bible at face value; it is a betrayal; a violation of the trust scripture bestows on its custodians. 1996

We should make no mistake: historical research does affect belief. 1996

Biblical scholars went indoors about 1923 and have refused to come out. We are closet scholars. Since the controversy over Darwin and evolution (*Origins of Species* published in 1869) erupted, we have been wary of public discourse. The Scopes trial taught us that it was dangerous to speak and write in plain language. . . . As a result of this case and similar controversies, biblical scholars learned to speak to and write for each other in codes that cannot be broken by the uninitiated. Like other academicians struggling for a place in the sun, we have made a virtue out of the trivial, articulated in bloated and esoteric rhetoric, and published in journals in which the footnote is king, in order to skirt or obscure the real issues. 1996

Since the object of the study of Greek is the use of the language rather than its mortification, the student is advised to devote his or her time to a mastery of the language rather than to a mastery of the grammar. 1973

The student (and teacher!) should keep a Greek text before him or her at all times. All learning should take place with an actual text in view. 1973

Every translation is a betrayal: it is misleading in some respects. But every translation is also a revelation. 1996

A translation is artful to the extent that one can forget, while reading it, that it is a translation at all. 1990

In an oral culture, plagiarism is an unknown category. Only in written cultures like our own has it become a moral and legal problem.

The literal-mindedness of the scientific age has also aggravated modern misunderstanding of ancient texts. There is a widespread notion that if Jesus did not say the words attributed to him, the gospels cannot be true. The truth of the gospels for many theologians does not depend on the accuracy of their quotations.   1991

Myth, Symbols, and Meaning

*W*e did not elect to pass from one age to another. We did not willfully abandon the symbols and myths that once served Western people well. But those symbols and myths are gone. They linger on, to be sure, in cultural eddies, especially in North America, owing to a receding level of literacy in both the Bible and the sciences. But they have lost their cogency.   2006

Because symbols and myths are social products, we cannot adopt or abandon them arbitrarily. But we can track their trajectories. It is worth knowing where we are in the life cycle of a symbol system.   2003

We can reform symbols but we cannot create them out of nothing and we cannot will their demise.   2002

As a tradition matures, its myths, symbols and lexical stock, its semantic logic, are crystallized. The meanings evoked by the terms of a culture are sedimented. The crystallization and sedimentation of a tradition constitute the immediate background within which and against which one speaks or writes the language. If one simply traffics in the sedimented tradition, one merely repeats what is already contained in the language. Under these circumstances, the text produced is rightly interpreted within the framework of the sedimented or dictionary meanings of the terms.   1975

The one thing that has not changed for us is that we still live by our myths.   2003

Theology

*P*aul is the first to attempt anything like ordered reflection on the meaning of Christian faith.   1968

It is quite possible that authentic theology in the future will be prosecuted in the secular university and/or in the parish church, especially the disestablished type.   1975

The divisions among the historical, systematic, and practical disciplines should be resolutely exorcized; the divisions do not represent a division of labor or the hermeneutical circle linking the past to the present, but three competing, political bases for theology, no one of which is any longer viable.   1975

The basis of the practical disciplines, which are patronizingly grounded in the needs of the churches, has become illegitimate because the needs of the church are no longer an index to anything significant.   1975

Every institution harboring the practice of theology should have cold beer on tap in its common room.   1975

The learning and teaching of theology require a new form of monasticism, in which intense, rigorous preoccupation with irrelevant things, such as a button discovered in the gutter, takes place in uncloistered precincts.   1975

All teachers and students of theology, and their near kin, should learn to fly-fish, wander in the wilderness, and bake bread.   1975

At the very least, theology must be rejoined to the sciences. We cannot afford another extended divorce.   1999

If theology is to address the human question, the study of theology ought to begin these days with a study of poetry—not a study of verse, but a study of poiesis in the root sense. Franz Kafka, Jorge Luis Borges, Albert Camus, Henry Miller, Samuel Beckett, Eugene Ionesco and their relatives may be sufficiently strong medicine to induce theology, once the queen of the humanities, to shake off her torpor. At all events, theology is uniquely prepared, by virtue of her history, to participate in preparing the way for the creation, recognition, and reception of liberating poiesis, if and when it comes, under whatever guise.   1975

The real theological issue is whether human beings can find a concrete context for their existence, a real world to which they can give themselves. And it is this *human* question to which theology must learn increasingly to devote itself.   1975

Cross

*I*n the Christian epic codified in the Apostles' Creed, the story of Jesus culminates in the cross, and the cross means that Christ died for our sins. The cross in that myth is indelibly linked to the understanding of Jesus' death as a sacrificial atonement. That link supports the church as a salvation machine which feeds on human guilt for its sustenance. And it is linked to the Christian claim that salvation is possible only under the sign of the cross. That claim is the legacy of Constantine and the feudal monarchy, now embodied in the Roman church. We can no longer tolerate either of these connotations of the cross. We must abandon and suppress them if the cross is to survive as symbol.   2002

The Jesus of the parables and aphorisms becomes the victim of his own vision; he dies with his trust in God inviolate; he has learned to be indifferent to life in the bosom of that trust. He frames his admonitions for himself; he tells his parables as though he were hearing them. The cross, in retrospect, is the symbol of that integrity. As Socrates chose to drink the hemlock rather than deny the law its due, so in a similar way the cross expresses Jesus' surrender to his vision. He was unwilling to compromise his vision for the sake of survival, for the sake of expediency, for the sake of success. Absolute, uncompromising integrity is the true meaning of the cross.   2002

Jesus was not merely a victim; he was the victim of his own vision. The cross for Jesus and the hemlock for Socrates are symbols of uncompromising integrity.   1996

The pre-eminent Christian symbol has come to be the cross. It was not always so. That investment began in earnest with Constantine in the fourth century and was renewed with interest in the Crusades. It haunts the relation of Christians to Jews. Mel Gibson has set Christianity back four hundred years by focusing exclusively on the cross in its bloodiest form as the symbol of Christianity. The film is deeply anti-Jewish, just as the gospels, especially John, are anti-Jewish. I see no way to eradicate this blemish on the Christian conscience other than to revise the gospels and replace the cross as the primary symbol.   2007

The word of grace is . . . the word of the cross. Jesus goes to the cross because he clings to the word of grace: that is at once the offense to the elder son and the hope of the younger. It is an offense to the older son because he, unlike Jesus, cannot give up his claim; it is the hope of the younger because he knows he has no claim. Those who hear the word of grace as a word addressed to them know the meaning of the cross. For just as Jesus invests everything, including whatever title he had a right to claim, as well as his life, in the certainty of that word of grace, so they who hear the word will know what it requires of them. By hearing they have been claimed as a vessel of grace and plunged into the way of the cross.   1966

Canon

I use the term "canon" in its broad, secular sense to refer to any collection of literature produced during the formative or golden age of a cultural tradition. In this extended definition, a canon need not be concerned with either "orthodoxy" or "heresy," only with the quality and variety of the emerging tradition.

Reference is frequently made to the Classical Canon or the canon of literature in English. Classical scholars do not talk about either orthodox or heretical works produced during the classical age of Greece; they speak only of works of higher or lesser quality, works that are more or less representative of the genius of the golden age of Greece. The twenty-six works Harold Bloom includes in his canon of great Western prose and poetry have nothing to do with what might be considered by some to be orthodox or heretical in great literature. This is the sense in which I use the "canon" of the literature of primitive Christianity.   2000

In a canonical work, Bloom writes, "you encounter a stranger, an uncanny startlement rather than a fulfillment of expectations." Strong poets startle and frighten because they invoke visions of worlds aborning, of vistas not accessible to the habituated perspectives of the everyday and ordinary. Their words cannot be assimilated to the received tradition, to what everybody already knows, because they have chosen them with such great care so as to offend, to disrupt, to bewitch, to charm, to enchant. Strong poets mark the turbulent transition to new worlds.   2000

Jesus and Paul are the only strong poets in the New Testament, the only authoritative voices, and they are the precipitators of the vision that produced the Christian movement. Yet, they have both been muffled by an oppressive overlay of mythic iconography and tables of received virtue. . . . The original deviations of Jesus and Paul have been brought to heel.   2000

Jesus was a strong poet. A strong poet startles us by opening up the world view. A strong poet modifies the way we see reality; he or she subverts the inherited symbolic universe.   2002

The canon of Christian literature should, I assume, have some connection, however remote, with Jesus of Nazareth, the alleged precipitator of the tradition that stems from him. This is the only absolute requisite for documents to be thought of as Christian. Beyond this fundamental criterion, selection should be based on the quality and variety of the voices that come to expression in written documents.   2000

To retain the New Testament as canon in its ancient sense is to condemn it to progressive irrelevance with each passing century.   2000

The canon of the New Testament was developed, along with the creeds, as a way of excluding political enemies, so regarded because they deviated from institutional opinion or practice; the primary interest was to build a fence around right doctrine and hierarchic privilege. This also had the effect of consolidating ecclesiastical power. The scholars of the Bible in the twentieth century—at least those who call themselves critical scholars—should have as their aim the desire to lay bare that process.   2006

To claim that the New Testament documents were both orthodox and inspired is to say the same thing. A book was thought to be inspired if it were orthodox, and orthodox if it were inspired. The employment of these two criteria is a tactical ploy: define as canonical what the bishops have decided is orthodox and declare it to be inspired at the same time; eliminate everything that does not fit the orthodox mold and you produce an impregnable circle.   2000

In spite of scholarly efforts to control the tradition, the old New Testament has long since ceased to be a canon: It lacks real authority in our society, even among, or perhaps especially among, scholars, despite protestations to the contrary. The common readers hear only what study Bibles permit him or her to hear. And scholars devise hermeneutics to support the party line: redaction criticism, reader response criticism, an eschatological Jesus positioned outside of space and time, who is now weightless and timeless, available for whatever service his worshipers need. That Jesus is no longer a threat to anyone or everything. Paul has suffered a similar fate. The Pastoral epistles have all but obscured the historical Paul; the Pauline school has turned Paul into a manual of church order.   2000

The Christian movement, contrary to popular opinion, was not a religion of the book from the beginning. It was, in fact, a movement of the spirit.   2000

The shift to writing goes together with the tendency to create something that is stable, crystallized, definitive—that can be handed around and on with ease. The very notion of canon presupposes tradition that is written. The transition from oral to written goes together with the move away from the free expression of the spirit to the controlled expression of bishops in an institution. It marks the transition from word *of* God to word *about* God.   2000

The canon of the early Christian movement is a spectrum of tradition and interpretation. The only question is whether the ancient councils and bishops narrowed the spectrum too much. They certainly did not expand it prodigally; yet they were wise enough to include a variety of documents in their lists of works recommended to be read in the churches; it was not a monolithic collection. It now appears that they were so exercised about heresy—read, their own authority and power—that they narrowed the spectrum too much both laterally and vertically. With respect to the lateral dimension, they failed to include a fully representative spectrum of memory and interpretation in their definition of "orthodoxy." As a consequence, the tradition soon became too incestuous and brittle to adapt itself to new contexts and problems. With regard to the vertical dimension, the tradition was cut off at an early date from some of its roots—the vision of Jesus was obscured by interpretive overlay and the authentic voice of Paul smothered by Pauline imitators. These deficiencies, unfortunately, cannot be entirely remedied since some of the founding documents have been destroyed.   2000

Academia

*T*here is good reason to believe that teaching and research are today being hampered, even strangled, by what someone has dramatically referred to as the knowledge explosion. This robust expression conjures up the mushroom cloud associated with Hiroshima and the Nevada desert. The happy consciousness triggered by this image has visions of imminent shock waves of instant progress and subsequent fallout of showers of scientific blessing. Yet even the ordinary soul in the street has a tinge of uneasiness: instant progress may do no more than aggravate the present ills of society, and those blessed showers may be laden with radioactive particles. In any case, the most rigorous intellects will suffocate when inundated by quantities of information too vast to be ingested, and the most devoted teachers will become antiquated when forced to leave their journals, however briefly, for a turn at the lectern.   1975

The humanities faculty has contributed, willy-nilly, to the growing incidence of illiteracy among university graduates. The classical tradition it is constrained to pass on is probably no longer within reach of the average, perhaps, not even of the advantaged, student. Who, save the expert, can read Homer or Dante, Virgil or Milton, with anything like the resonances available to a grammar school graduate of a century ago? It does not seem promising to begin an interpretation of the parable of the Samaritan with a disquisition on the history of the Samaritans. Yet the student can do with no less. . . . The allusions of T.S. Eliot exceed the grasp of most English majors. As glossaries expand and commentaries lengthen, the text is buried more and more under an avalanche of pedantic propaedeutic.   1975

The spoken word may be dying in order to be reborn. The symbolism of mathematics, the innovative and malleable forms of the new visual and auditory arts, all of which appear currently more powerful than their verbal counterparts, may contribute to the rebirth of images and ultimately to the rise of a regenerate rhetoric. Meanwhile, the university requires its Pentecost. The prophet is needed who can speak so that all may hear in his or her own idiom. The quarter from which help ought to be imminent is music, the language of the soul. Translation is not necessary, even for Martians. Beyond music lie the visual arts. Humanists and scientists alike could cluster around the holy pair and find a mutual eye and ear. Perhaps that is the only means of checking the final confusion of tongues, the ultimate silence.   1975

Deans and principals should enlist good teachers and promising students and then let them alone to perform their tasks.   1975

Teachers should afford students the same scholarly freedom they grant themselves, and should demand of students the same standards as they demand of themselves: what they do not give to and expect from students they will soon not give to and expect from themselves. The student, like the importunate widow, should worry the teacher until the student has the allegedly self-evident point well in hand: such persistence in students redounds not only to their own benefit, but to that of their teachers as well.   1975

A reliable guide to what is worthy of attention amidst the deluge of printed matter that assaults the optical nerves is alone worth the price of tuition.   1975

The professional put down is taken and mistaken for an academic mark up.   1989

I came to see that my academic colleagues and I were trapped in a perpetual holding pattern dictated to us by a system of rewards and sanctions in the university. That system prevented us, or at least discouraged us, from entering the public domain with learning that mattered. In their book, *The Social Construction of Reality*, Berger and Luckman define intellectuals as experts whose specialized knowledge is not wanted, is not even tolerated, by the general public. We have defined ourselves as intellectuals and glory in the fact that what we produce is of no real interest or obvious use to anyone outside other specialists. 1990

I weep to think that I spent thirty-five years in the classroom, in concert with thousands of other colleagues, to have had so little lasting impact on undergraduates, ministerial students, and the American mind. Religious literacy has reached a new low in spite of our scholarship, in spite of our domination of the college and university system, in spite of the remarkable advances in research and publication our academic disciplines have made. 1990

The biggest challenge of all is to package our product—the fruit of research and deliberations—in a form or forms that will make it readily accessible to our clients and that will attract the public's attention. For scholars this is perhaps the most formidable—and threatening—challenge of all. 1990

The great thinkers and scientists of the Enlightenment were essentially propagandists. They wrote for the general reader. I think that is what has worried me most about the loss of a public base for scholars of religion, for scholars of the humanities generally. 2004

Universities are much like churches, replete with orthodoxies of various kinds, courts of inquisition, and severe penalties for those who do not embrace mediocrity and the teachers' union. 1996

In the academic world, penalties are severe for the author who writes a book that sells well, or for sponsors of the lucid sentence, or for teachers who can teach but fail to publish. Promotion and tenure committees look askance at such successes: after all, if a work is well written and elicits a broad readership, if a sentence is understandable, if students actually learn, that scholarship cannot be very profound. The inevitable result is that academics deliberately write in convoluted jargon merely to please their elitist colleagues. 1996

Scholars are basically the recipients of patronage. They are, in fact, clients of broker deans and committees on promotion and tenure and behave much like enslaved intellectuals. They have mortgaged most of their freedom to think and act as they please or as their research dictates. Tenure for them means job security rather than independence. They pretend to exercise unfettered judgments about important matters, but do so mostly when that exercise doesn't count for much or when it is merely a fashion statement. 1996

Most of us learned to answer questions posed by students with the dodge: we lectured around the issue rather than come straight to the unvarnished point. Perhaps that is the wiser course for the immature student. But it does engender duplicity of mind. The almost universal tendency of theologians when speaking publicly is to say one thing understood in conventional terms while intending something quite different. 2002

Universities and learned societies, like corporations, need advisors, including professional managers, who have nothing to gain in the success of the venture. A board made up entirely of those whose self-interest is at stake is not able to make decisions that transcend their own personal stakes in the business. 2002

The bureaucracy of a learned society is necessary but an evil. Accordingly, it is to be cultivated and pruned, simultaneously, like vines. Bureaucracy is poison: there should be as little as possible, but what there is should be potent. 1973

The leaders of a learned society should be measured, not by the specific achievements of their tenure, but by the stature of the people required to replace them. 1973

Officers entering upon their tenure are required to plan and project. Retiring officials are permitted to prophesy. The difference is that the first may be held accountable for promises, the latter are merely indulged. Fortunately, the latter may also be ignored. 1973

The humanistic learned society has too long remained a gentlemen's debating club, with tables for ladies.   1971

The Society of Biblical Literature is a fraternity of scientifically trained biblical scholars with the soul of a church.   1976

Libraries, Books, and Journals

*T*he primary loci of the production of knowledge are and remain the private study, the library, the research institute and laboratory, and the graduate seminar, all predominantly in a college or university context.   1976

Since the scholar must start over with the eccentricities of the institutional library to which he or she moves, more weight has to be placed on the private collection.   1978

The institutional library is becoming as embattled as the private scholarly library, and for much the same reasons. Since academic libraries account for 60 to 70 per cent of the market in scholarly books, the retrenchment of university libraries has adversely affected the entire cycle: books are not being purchased and journals are being discontinued. Even the New York Public Library has joined the soup line.   1978

Most scholars are nostalgic about the private library once the hallmark of the serious scholar. They have not given up book buying of their own volition; they have been driven from it by outrageous prices designed to recover costs from the first wave of institutional sales.   1973

The day may come when it will no longer be any advantage at all to live across the yard from Widener Library.   1971

For Kafka, "a book must be an ice-axe to break the frozen sea around us." With such books in such hands, the library would be closed down as the seedbed of revolutions, and the university would not long survive its present decadent form.   1975

The journal is the battleground of the birth and death of ideas and methodologies. 1976

Teacher and student should never be more than arm's length from the cream of what has been written (institutional libraries should be distributed to locations where teachers and students spend the bulk of their time). 1975

It is often said that periodicals represent the growing edge of scholarship, monographs the fruit of mature reflection, while encyclopedias are monuments to a preceding age. 1964

We too often mistake the number of secondary references and abstruse vocabulary in essays and books for high scholarship. The best scholarship is lucid. It is lucid because it deals with the foundations, which clamor eternally for renewal. And if we have not gotten lost in the forest of our pedantry, we will be addressing questions that concern our public, even though that public may not be aware of the connection. 1989

Scholars once copied their works by hand, or had them copied by apprentices and professional scribes. They were overseers of the process firsthand. In modern times, scholars have become divorced from the means of publication and dissemination, to the detriment of both. Some restoration of the relation between and among scholars, publishers, printers and pressmen, and librarians is essential to understanding and co-operation. 1978

Scholarly publishing is a dependent activity: it lives off the academic process. But it also nurtures that process at the same time. Scholarly publishers will flourish to the extent that they maintain the health of their host; the two are twins with a single life-support system. 1978

Authorship in the modern sense—which is what makes plagiarism possible—belongs to a print culture. 1987

Learning

*A*cquiring a degree, even from a first-rate university, does not make one learned or wise. 2002

The acquisition of information is no certain cure of ignorance. 2002

Learning is an adventure. It is a quest for the holy grail of truth, that elusive treasure which everyone seeks but no one can really possess. 2002

Learning new truths can be excruciating, but learning can also be filled with visits to strange new domains and exciting fresh experiences. Pain and suffering are the companions of joy and satisfaction in the quest for truth. . . . I have never known progress to be free of pain. 2002

Learning is a contest—a contest with ourselves as the chief opponent, with the superficial, entrenched ideas we have acquired from the popular culture around us and even from our parents and grandparents. In Greek the word for contest (*agon*) is the same word from which we get the term "agony": learning is agony. Learning the truth about the Jewish and Christian traditions that stem from the Bible can be the most agonizing of all exercises. 2002

My own intellectual and religious odyssey has been filled with agony. At the same time, it has brought me deep satisfactions. I have gone looking for what can be known, what can be discovered and explored, openly, joyfully, satisfyingly. If I could sing, I would add, accompanied by singing. 2002

I taught in university and seminary classrooms for nearly forty years. My initial warning to students who signed up for my classes was this: stay away from the library. Don't read the books and essays I will assign you. The library is filled with subversive literature: great books are designed to undermine your smug views of the world. The best minds may awaken you to vistas you did not know existed. Your world may be shaken to the foundations. 2002

One of the things I have learned from serving on promotion and tenure committees in universities is that it is a sin to write a popular book; if it sells well, it isn't profound. It is equally a sin to write a profound book. To gain approval from our colleagues we must write mediocre books. 2002

I learned eventually that the secular university is not much different from the divinity school. The faculty, like Gaul, is divided into three parts: the religiously conservative; the skeptics who abhor religion and things religious; and the educated. 2002

In a general way, the move from priest to teacher to artist marks the retreat from an ordinary, certified, guaranteed, comfortable reality toward a non-ordinary, indeterminate, surprising form of world. For the priest, reality is revealed; it is unnecessary to discover the real for oneself. For the teacher, reality is rational; one discovers the real by reason. For the artist, on the other hand, what is commonly assumed to be real is illusory; the everyday world is phony. The artist in this trinity is not necessarily a painter or sculptor. The artist stands for all those who think they are hemmed in by the false, by archaic assumptions, by fabricated boundaries that insulate from the real. 2002

The beginning of knowledge is knowing the right questions to ask. 1996

I discovered that real learning is *agony*—a struggle, a contest with ourselves, with superficial, entrenched ideas, and with the lore we absorb from the surrounding cultural atmosphere. Learning the truth about the Christian tradition can be the most agonizing of all exercises.   1996

Søren Kierkegaard, the melancholy Dane, once wisely observed that we live life forward but understand it backwards. Our basic task as graduates of an institution of higher learning is to extrapolate a future from what we have learned about our past.   2005

I had the good fortune of playing basketball under legendary coast Tony Hinkle at Butler University. I learned from Coach Hinkle that basketball is a *team* sport. He taught us that any five players acting as a unit were superior to another five acting as individuals. It was a lesson I took to heart. "I belong to the team; therefore I am" was the beginning of my self-definition.   2005

If you haven't done so already, you will need to learn that the acquisition of knowledge and the development of new products and theories are increasingly the result of team efforts. If you should have the good fortune to lead a team in the quest for new knowledge, surround yourself with people who are at least as smart and clever as you are, and who have the strength of character not to be misled by your charm.   2005

Wisdom is the ability to manage the transitions we will make in life with equanimity because we have surrounded ourselves with good companions and friends.   2005

Acute self-transcendence is the epitome of wisdom. I like this reminder I saw on a bumper sticker: Jesus loves you; everyone else thinks you're a jerk. That little gem restores equilibrium to our self-assessment.   2006

I write principally to find out what I think, or aspire to think, and so am my own first reader. . . . I am not infrequently amazed and often amused at what I write. The delete key on my computer is a close friend.   1996

Humor

*T*here is a kind of humor in fundamentalism, but that humor is rarely self-directed; it is nearly always aimed at the enemy. Humor for me is primarily a good laugh at self-importance, at one's own foibles, at pomposity, at pretension, at arrogance. As a consequence, I have never been prompted to laugh with Jerry Falwell; I am always tempted to laugh at him. That is not the best form of humor.   2002

The affliction of much contemporary religiosity, especially of the moralistic variety, is that it is humorless. If we cannot laugh at ourselves and even about the things we hold dear, then God's reign has eluded us.   2002

Our investigations, our quest for truth, should be sprinkled with humor. We must not take ourselves too seriously. As serious as this business of the bible and Jesus and religion is, we should remember that we are all buffoons of one sort or another, clowns strutting about on life's stage or waiting in the wings, as Paul suggests in his second letter to the Corinthians.   1996

Jesus makes free use of parody. The parable of the empty jar in the Gospel of Thomas is a parody of the jar of meal miraculously replenished by Elijah for the widow of Zarepath. The Mustard Seed pokes fun at the image of the mighty cedar of Lebanon employed by Ezekiel as a symbol for the mighty kingdom of David.

Parody is a form of humor, to be sure. But Jesus indulges in other forms of humor. In the parable of the lost coin, the woman spends the value of the coin she has just recovered in celebrating her good fortune. The shepherd recovers the lost sheep and promptly announces a celebration, which probably involved the slaughter of a sheep. When sued for your coat, Jesus advises his followers, to give up your shirt to go with it. That would of course leave them naked. Jesus' listeners must have laughed at these travesties on sober speech.   2002

Jesus' saying about giving up one's shirt to go with a coat claimed under the law would have been a howler in a two-garment society.   2002

What goes in, he says, cannot defile, but what comes out can and does. He doesn't specify which orifice in the human body he has in mind. We know that the first has to refer to the mouth, since that is the primary opening through which things are taken in. He thus declares that no foods are unclean. On the other hand, it is the lower orifice in a society without plumbing that is the source of most pollution. By contrasting the upper with the lower orifice, Jesus may have been indulging in a bit of humor to make an important point.   2002

Humor in most of its forms is inimical to morality. Moralisms are the enemy of humor.   1999

Humor prevents us from becoming doctrinaire; ambiguity inhibits dogmatism. Moreover, humor and humility are twins. Humor is the antidote for arrogance and hubris. Most of all, we will avoid moralistic pronouncements if we speak with tongue in cheek.   1999

John is deadly and consequently tiring. Jesus is funny and therefore interesting.   1968

Quips

*M*y definition of leadership: Find a parade and get in front of it.

All my plans are written in water.

Everyone should have a Plan B.

I just love to shake things up.

I like administration. It's a way to ensure that things get done.

The standard bureaucrat confuses the habitual "no" with the power to discriminate.

Charting after the fact permits the navigator to omit mention of storms, drift, and faulty compass readings.

At the hearth one must be keenly alert to the danger of falling statuary: there one is prompted to inspect the household gods.

I taught you. You just forgot.

Just call me Bob.

Favorite Aphorisms

*W*e wouldn't be so concerned about what people thought of us, if we realized how seldom they do. —Oscar Wilde

Flannery O'Connor was asked over and over again if she thinks the universities stifle writers. Her response, "Perhaps, but they don't stifle enough of them."

Harry Luccock, who taught homiletics at Yale University for many years was once asked, "How many points should a sermon have?" To the question, he replied, "At least one."

Faith for the Future

*W*e need to conceive a faith that reconciles our need to know historically and scientifically with our need to create symbols and form myths. That means we must explore the parameters of a faith inspired by Jesus on a much broader front, including the biological, environmental, psychological, and social sciences. And we must include architecture and the arts, visual and aural, as well as performing.   2001

The problem we face is that God is not a primary datum. God is derivative of the human imagination. We do not know God directly; no one has seen God, or heard or smelled God. Those who claim to know God can only give us an account of their experiences. An experience of God, or a revelation from God, is an interpreted experience, since there is no such thing as an uninterpreted experience. It seems we have invented God in our own image.   2001

While the sciences, medicine, and technology are developing apace, the humanities and the spiritual disciplines are lagging. We need a new symbolic universe to replace the old one, along with a community for whom it becomes the paramount reality. It will not survive without community.   2003

When history is viewed as an evolutionary process, the past is stripped of its normative character.   1976

The New Testament, suitable for the third millennium, should include whatever traces of the original strangeness of Jesus and Paul we can isolate or reconstruct. As Bultmann once suggested, excavate to the foundations—

> Save nothing that does not preserve fragments of the initiating, unsettling, disruptive dreams.

Admit that Jesus died precisely for a few provocative witticisms and a handful of subversive short stories that leave us
gasping for breath at every reading.

Applaud Paul for the agonizing struggle with his own
Pharisaic past, the Paul who caught sight of the boundaryless community with no social barriers separating female
from male, Gentile from Jew, slave from free, black from
white, homosexual from heterosexual.

Reinstate the prophetic insight that Satan has been cast out of
heaven and the demonic powers subdued.

Recover the shocking notion that access to the divine does
not require brokers, that life is to be celebrated, that trust is
nectar of the gods.

These are the provocative features of those who caught a
glimpse of God's domain once upon a time.   2000

In the face of the modern paramount reality, what is left of the
historic Christian faith? That is a trenchant question. On my view,
just about everything important is left.   2003

With maturity comes the possibility of genuine fantasy, the possibility of religion.   1992

In Missoula, Montana, on Helen Avenue, not far from my former
home, is a Tolkien tree, a willow, to which I have become attached
because I always perceive it as the old willow on the Withywindle
River, not far from Tom Bombadil's home in the Old Forest. Tolkien
has woven that old tree into the fabric of his tale. His fantasy has
affected my perception of the willow and Helen Avenue forever.

At the same time, the new vision we acquire from fantasy frees
us from the calculating clutches of science and business: my Tolkien
tree is no longer so many board feet of lumber; it is a living being
with whom I may converse. As a new vision of things, fantasy may
afford a glimpse of the really real world, the hidden truth, that lies
beyond the horizon of present sight: the all-encompassing vision
that unites heaven and earth in one meaningful whole.

Fantasy can be a subversive instrument. It can undermine our
sense of things. We should therefore be circumspect in choosing

the fantasies with which we want to take up. The American mono-myth may in fact be lulling us to sleep because it depends on an external savior who will rise to our rescue at the last moment. Our real need is perhaps to be awakened so we can pass from adoles-cence to maturity. For this purpose, the fantasies of Hansel & Gretel and the Lord of the Rings are more promising fare than the Lone Ranger. 1992

I am filled with nostalgia for the twentieth century. I have lived most of my life in that century. I don't want to see it end. Yet, my head and heart belong to the nineteenth century, just as my aspi-rations and hope are focused on the twenty-first. I am a bundle of competing agendas. I am a conservative—I want to hang on to the best of the past. I am also a liberal—I am open to and ready to embrace the oncoming future. The agenda I must follow, however, is the one set for me by the present time. 1993

As we make the transition to the new age, the scriptures once thought to be the epitome of Christianity will look increasingly quaint, like a lacquered icon that has survived from some long lost world. Nevertheless, buried in the pages of those ancient docu-ments is a vision of the world as God's domain that once turned the whole of the Western world in a new direction. Those who treasure that vision must ask themselves whether they can retain that vision while shedding the remnants of a worldview whose archaic values and mythology are no longer viable. It is a formidable challenge to the church and all the members of the church alumni association, as Bishop Spong calls them. And it is a labor of love to everyone—church-connected or not—who has caught a glimpse of what Jesus of Nazareth was all about. 2000

I began quite young with a string of beliefs and very little faith. 1996

Spiritually I have gradually exchanged my youthful convictions for a certain amount of faith. By faith I do not mean "belief"; I mean "trust." The confusion, in popular usage, of faith as trust with faith as belief in a set of propositions has almost made the term in its proper sense unusable. In spite of progress, I still have trouble acting as though I trust that things will work out. I continue to be anxious about what I will eat and wear. I don't trust the people who are in charge, and I tend to let that distrust spill over into the cosmos. There are many days when I am inclined to reorganize things for God. Most of the time I have doubts that truth will be victorious, that the innocent won't suffer, that good will triumph over evil. . . .

Yet there are rare instances when I recognize that what I think is important may not in fact be significant, that I may not understand what truth is all about, and that the values I cherish may not be worth much. It is tough to have faith when the evidence doesn't support your private convictions. But then, that is what faith is—toughness in the face of rampant confusion and contrary evidence. 1996

Most of us . . . long for an external redeemer, the one who comes from another world and does for us what we are unable or unwilling to do for ourselves. We want a superman, or a wonder woman, or a King Arthur, or a John Wayne, or the hero with a thousand faces. But that messiah hasn't come and won't come. While we wait, rehearsing apocalyptic scenarios, the crisis deepens.

The messiah we need is some random act of kindness, some bold proposal to close the hole in the ozone, some discrete move to introduce candor into politics, some new intensive care for the planet. Perhaps the messiah will come when we have broken bread with our enemies. 1999

The Jesus tradition in its original form was metaphorical and non-literal and therefore not simply transmittable as words. Mere repetition of metaphors is deadening. Loving traditions have to be restated, retranslated, and reinterpreted in new and different contexts. Only in that way do they remain alive and thriving. 2003

What we need now is a faith to bridge our need to know scientifically and historically and our need to form symbols and create myths. 2003

A new vision will emerge in the imaginations of storytellers and poets, artists and architects, and perhaps even a theologian or two. 2003

Visions do not come to us whole. They come in fragments, glimpses, glimmerings, caught in the tail of the eye. . . . Spirituality in our time consists in glimpse training.   2003

If God has a role in the new vision, it will be as a metaphor. As a metaphor God can function as an integrating symbol. As a metaphor, God is a symbol that unites or encompasses all spheres of our reality. There is nothing that falls outside the single divine domain. Mystical visions regularly confirm that the universe is one, that it really is a universe and not a multiverse.   2003

As a metaphor, God must represent some dimension of human experience. Let me suggest four such dimensions.

First, God is the symbol for acute self-transcendence. We are inclined to deceive ourselves, to hide from the truth. An omniscient God reminds that we cannot hide. God knows everything; God will find us out. That is a very useful symbol that points beyond ordinary self-consciousness, and thus to a critical dimension of human experience.

Second, God is a metaphor for the oncoming future, for the fund of possibilities the future lays on the present. Because we live into our futures, God is the invitation to explore those possibilities and make the most of them.

Third, God is also the metaphor for a revisionist past. The old terms for this were forgiveness and redemption. God stands for the second chance. Because God is omnipotent, God can undo the past, provide us with the opportunity to start over.

Finally, God is the metaphor for the Beyond of the beyond. We know that we will eventually acquire new knowledge that will change present perspectives. . . . A few physicists today think they may be close to the fundamental building blocks of reality. That may be no more than scientific hubris. God also stands for the ultimate limit, the final horizon, the Beyond that we will never see. . . . God guards us from ultimate temptation: the temptation to think we are gods ourselves.   2003

God is also a metaphor for immanence. Immanence expresses the idea that, in spite of God's transcendence, the divine is nevertheless intimately related to the world. . . . Christian theologians have been in the habit of saying, if you want to know what God is like, look at Jesus of Nazareth. We now know that Jesus is not literally God. Yet Jesus allegedly represents the way God is related to the world. Both the acts and words of Jesus have been taken as indicators of the character of God. When the fathers of the church developed content for the character of God, they did not consult their abstract Christological formulations; they consulted the words and deeds of Jesus.   2003

Jesus experiences God, not as remote from the world, but as everywhere present in the most ordinary events.   2003

Jesus' vision of the world as God's domain is global in its reach. By insisting that to cling to life is to lose life, his vision transcends self-interest. He advocates love of the enemy, which means that God's domain transcends the tribe, the ethnic groups, and the nation. He no longer sponsors the male patriarch who dominates the family. He embraces all genders and ages. His notion of the kingdom is transhuman since it includes the birds and the flowers.

His views are transbiblical, transchristian, and even transreligious. He seems not to be bound by what the Bible says, and I see nothing in his vision that calls for a parochial religion like "churchianity." He appears not to require religion at all.   2003

We yearn for continued existence after death, though we don't know what to do with ourselves on a rainy Sunday afternoon.   1996

Christianity has turned its conviction about the resurrection of Jesus into the promise of an extended existence for all believers.   1996

Some will not agree, but I think Christianity is a tradition worth reforming and saving.   1996

The future of the Christian faith may turn out to be a minor aspect of the cultural shifts that are shaping our global future. The themes that have dominated the institutional churches may no longer be of central concern to us. But no matter. Yet at the heart of the old faith tradition there are topics and themes that are central to the human condition and the fate of the planet in the next millennium. Our task is to locate those themes and set them in a new and broader context.

Finally, it is well to remind ourselves that our task is not messianic. It may turn out not to be very important. Yet we must act on what we know, or think we know, at this moment in history. To do anything less would be to betray the faith we have.   2001

Twenty-one Theses

T wenty-one Theses

Theology

1. The God of the metaphysical age is dead. There is not a personal god out there external to human beings and the material world. We must reckon with a deep crisis in god talk and replace it with talk about whether the universe has meaning and whether human life has purpose.

2. The doctrine of special creation of the species died with the advent of Darwinism and the new understanding of the age of the earth and magnitude of the physical universe. Special creation goes together with the notion that the earth and human beings are at the center of the galaxy (the galaxy is anthropocentric). The demise of a geocentric universe took the doctrine of special creation with it.

3. The deliteralization of the story of Adam and Eve in Genesis brought an end to the dogma of original sin as something inherited from the first human being. Death is not punishment for sin, but is entirely natural. And sin is not transmitted from generation to generation by means of male sperm, as suggested by Augustine.

4. The notion that God interferes with the order of nature from time to time in order to aid or punish is no longer credible, in spite of the fact that most people still believe it. Miracles are an affront to the justice and integrity of God, however understood. Miracles are conceivable only as the inexplicable; otherwise they contradict the regularity of the order of the physical universe.

5. Prayer is meaningless when understood as requests addressed to an external God for favor or forgiveness and meaningless

if God does not interfere with the laws of nature. Prayer as praise is a remnant of the age of kingship in the ancient Near East and is beneath the dignity of deity. Prayer should be understood principally as meditation—as listening rather than talking—and as attention to the needs of neighbor.

Christology

6. We should give Jesus a demotion. It is no longer credible to think of Jesus as divine. Jesus' divinity goes together with the old theistic way of thinking about God.

7. The plot early Christians invented for a divine redeemer figure is as archaic as the mythology in which it is framed. A Jesus who drops down out of heaven, performs some magical act that frees human beings from the power of sin, rises from the dead, and returns to heaven is simply no longer credible. The notion that he will return at the end of time and sit in cosmic judgment is equally incredible. We must find a new plot for a more credible Jesus.

8. The virgin birth of Jesus is an insult to modern intelligence and should be abandoned. In addition, it is a pernicious doctrine that denigrates women.

9. The doctrine of the atonement—the claim that God killed his own son in order to satisfy his thirst for satisfaction—is subrational and subethical. This monstrous doctrine is the stepchild of a primitive sacrificial system in which the gods had to be appeased by offering them some special gift, such as a child or an animal.

10. The resurrection of Jesus did not involve the resuscitation of a corpse. Jesus did not rise from the dead, except perhaps in some metaphorical sense. The meaning of the resurrection is that a few of his followers—probably no more than two or three—finally came to understand what he was all about. When the significance of his words and deeds dawned on them, they knew of no other terms in which to express their amazement than to claim that they had seen him alive.

11. The expectation that Jesus will return and sit in cosmic judgment is part and parcel of the mythological worldview that is now defunct. Furthermore, it undergirds human lust for the

punishment of enemies and evildoers and the corresponding hope for rewards for the pious and righteous. All apocalyptic elements should be expunged from the Christian agenda.

God's Domain According to Jesus

12. Jesus advocated and practiced a trust ethic. The kingdom of God, for Jesus, is characterized by trust in the order of creation and the essential goodness of neighbor.

13. Jesus urges his followers to celebrate life as though they had just discovered a cache of coins in a field or been invited to a state banquet.

14. For Jesus, God's domain is a realm without social boundaries. In that realm there is neither Jew nor Greek, male nor female, slave nor free, homosexual nor heterosexual, friend nor enemy.

15. For Jesus, God's domain has no brokers, no mediators between human beings and divinity. The church has insisted on the necessity of mediators in order to protect its brokerage system.

16. For Jesus, the kingdom does not require cultic rituals to mark the rites of passage from outsider to insider, from sinner to righteous, from child to adult, from client to broker.

17. In the kingdom, forgiveness is reciprocal: individuals can have it only if they sponsor it.

18. The kingdom is a journey without end: one arrives only by departing. It is therefore a perpetual odyssey. Exile and exodus are the true conditions of authentic existence.

The Canon

19. The New Testament is a highly uneven and biased record of orthodox attempts to invent Christianity. The canon of scripture adopted by traditional Christianity should be contracted and expanded simultaneously to reflect respect for the old tradition and openness to the new. Only the works of strong poets—those who startle us, amaze us with a glimpse of what lies beyond the rim of present sight—should be considered for inclusion. The canon should be a collection of scriptures,

without a fixed text and without either inside or outside limits, like the myth of King Arthur and the knights of the roundtable or the myth of the American West.

20. The Bible does not contain fixed, objective standards of behavior that should govern human behavior for all time. This includes the ten commandments as well as the admonitions of Jesus.

The Language of Faith

21. In rearticulating the vision of Jesus, we should take care to express ourselves in the same register as he employed in his parables and aphorisms—paradox, hyperbole, exaggeration, and metaphor. Further, our reconstructions of his vision should be provisional, always subject to modification and correction.   1998

Final Words

*W*hat binds us together is care for the truth, for each other, and for the earth that is our home. The symbol of this new extended family is the open table. Seated around that table, breaking bread together, one may occasionally catch sight of God's domain, somewhere just beyond the horizon.   1999

The vision of Jesus, when translated into terms appropriate to our own time and place, moves from our present of unfulfilled promises to a future of partially realized hopes within a horizon of trust. That vision offers some hope for our collective future on planet earth, especially if taken in concert with the wisdom of other sages and visionaries from our own and other cultures.   2003

The real Jesus escapes now and again from the scriptural and creedal prisons in which we entomb him. He asserts his freedom from the claims we have made on his behalf. He refuses our honors, our adoration, and he charts his own course.

But the worshipers of Jesus will take him prisoner once again, crucify him all over again, and seal him once more in his tomb. Easter morning means that he will escape perpetually into some new horizon and violate some new boundary marker. When he does so, he will liberate us from the windowless cells we inhabit and introduce us to worlds that lie beyond the rim of present sight.   1993

It is time to take a walk and come to one's senses. Or it may be a time to go fishing where a river runs through it.   1975

For Further Reading

Books by Robert W. Funk

Honest to Jesus: Jesus for a New Millennium. San Francisco: HarperSanFrancisco, 1996.

> The best overview of Funk's thought, ranging from the historical Jesus and the authenticity of the gospels to his vision of Jesus and Christianity for the new millennium. More importantly, "it is a manifesto that declares with unflinching confidence that critical, honest, public scholarship matters" (Stephen J. Patterson).

A Credible Jesus: Fragments of a Vision. Santa Rosa, CA: Polebridge Press, 2002.

> Jesus' vision comes in random stunning insights, embedded in the everyday language of his parables, aphorisms, and dialogues. Funk sorts and assembles these fragments and examines ways in which the vision they preserve can serve twenty-first century people searching for meaning in a very different world than the one Jesus inhabited.

The Five Gospels: The Search for the Authentic Words of Jesus (with Roy W. Hoover and the Jesus Seminar). New York: Macmillan, 1993.

> The best-selling volume that documents the first major project of The Jesus Seminar. Some 75 scholars collaboratively assessed the authenticity of the more than 1,500 sayings attributed to Jesus. Each saying is famously color-coded and presented in a completely new translation of the Greek and Coptic texts, with an illuminating commentary.

The Jesus Seminar

Reports and articles prepared for the general reader are printed in *The Fourth R: An Advocate for Religious Literacy* (ISSN 0893–1658) which is published bi-monthly. The Jesus Seminar publishes its technical papers in *Forum*, a scholarly journal (ISSN 0883–4970). Both publications are under the auspices of the Westar Institute and published by Polebridge Press, Santa Rosa, California (www. westarinstitute.org).

Citations

The citations are in page number order and are keyed to the Abbreviations and Works Cited sections that follow.

3, Jesus experiences God, FoP, 194

3, Jesus never refers, IC, 22

3, Jesus did not, FoP, 172; cf. GoJ 8 and JNG, 18

3, Jesus rejected, JNG, 18

3, The old God, FoP 185–86

4, The final nail, FoP, 190

5, We have been slow, FoP, 177

5, God may continue, FoP, 191

9, The quest of the historical Jesus is a quest, HtJ, 29

9, The quest of the historical Jesus is an effort, HtJ, 31

9, To describe Jesus, JaP, 140

9, Critical scholars, CJ, 4

9, Individuals and institutions, JTW, 1

10, In order to pursue, JTW, 1–2

10, It may be thought, FoP, 164

10, David Friedrich Strauss', FoP, 180

10, In public controversies, HJB, 13

11. The resolution of the argument, OFJ, 23

11, The discrepancy, IC, 28

11, We will never, EJ, 10–11

11, Critical Questions, EJ, 15

12, Criteria for Determining, CfD, 9–10

12, I share an interest, HtJ, 18–19

12, The real reason, HtJ, 19

13, The Jesus movement, HtJ, 20

13, If we cannot reach, HtJ, 21

13, Neo-orthodox theologians, HtJ, 63

13, In the Gospel of John, HtJ, 127

17, Jesus fraternized openly, JNG, 18

17, The pale, anemic, JNG, 17

17, Like other exorcists, JNG, 18

17, Jesus' vision, SME, 18

17, Jesus enjoined subversive, JTW, 6

18, The gospel Jesus proclaimed, GoJ, 3

18, In a well-ordered society, GoJ, 5

18, The wall around temples, GoJ, 5

19, Jesus practiced and advocated, JNG, 19

19, The gospel of Jesus, JNG, 6

19, On the basis, FoP, 166

19, In his brief references, FoP, 167

19, A close examination, GoJ, 7

19, The narrative gospels, GoJ, 7

19, Jesus did not ask, GoJ, 8

19, Jesus had nothing, HtJ, 41–42

20, Readers of the gospels, FoP, 166

20, Jesus is a heroic figure, HtJ, 170

20, The new Jesus, GoJ, 10

20, Jesus has become, OFJ, 22

21, Jesus of Nazareth, IC, 36

21, The gospels can be said, HJB, 12

21, Jesus denied his followers, JNG, 19

21, Jesus' vision consisted, IC, 19

21, If the gap, IC, 19

21, The gospel of Jesus, IC, 22

21, Reality is fabulous, JaP, 88

22, Jesus' language, EJ, 11

22, The narrative contexts, EJ, 11

22, Jesus' assessment of himself, EJ, 12

22, Had Jesus lived, EJ, 14

22, Jesus had no idea, EJ, 15

23, Visions come in bits, CJ, 2

23, Jesus' vision did not have, CJ, 12

23, We can think, CJ, 15; cf. FoP, 174; cf. JNG, 19

23, Wisdom is not concerned, OFJ, 15

23, Sages often embrace, CJ, 48

23, Some of his followers, CJ, 16

103, Unlike Jesus and Paul, SBC, 362

104, The New Testament, IC, 38

104, To listen to, HtJ, 52–53

104, The King James Version, HtJ, 81

107, David Koresh, GEW, 14

107, In our time, HtJ, 5–6

107, Too many Americans, Ltr

108, Ignorance breeds bigotry, OFJ, 6

108, Jesus helped people, OFJ, 19

108, Biblical literacy often, OFJ, 20

111, The popular Christian, CJ, 24

111, Few in our society, GEW, 15

111, We know that, IC, 38

111, [The Book of] Revelation, JA, 7

111, The surface of the earth, JA, 3; EF, 28

111, Those who claim, JA, 3; cf. FoP, 192

111, The view that, EJ, 11; cf. JTW, 2

112, The apocalyptic visions, JA, 7

112, The apocalyptic hope, JTW, 2; cf. EJ, 11

112, When Jesus advises, JaP, 108; cf. FoP, 169

112, The apocalyptic tradition, OFJ 13

115, Scholars of the gospels, HtJ, 179; cf. FoP, 117

115, Scholars have a taste, BCO, 10

115, Because the question, WAB, 21

115, I am proposing, IJ, 7

116, It is clear, TM1, 2

116, Where have all, WHA, 8

116, Our scholarship, TM1, 1–2

116, It is profoundly, TM1, 6

116, We deliberately put, TM1, 2

117, Our concentration on, TM1, 6

117, One of the powerful, TM2, 4

117, Insulated and isolated, HtJ, 6

117, Biblical criticism, CaO, 388

117, Rightly dividing, OFJ, 21

117, The church bureaucracy, IC, 45

118, Methodology is not, FoP, 94

118, We can no longer, ICr, 15

118, The strength and vitality, HtJ, 21

118, How the scholarly, HtJ, 22

119, We should make no, HtJ, 23

119, Biblical scholars, HtJ, 54–55

119, Since the object, BIG, xxviii

119, The student (and teacher), BIG, xxix

119, Every translation, HtJ, 81

119, A translation is artful, CSS, 12

120, In an oral culture, PRS, 2

123, We did not elect, FoP, 178

123, Because symbols, FoP, 178; cf. EF, 30

123, We can reform, CJ, 141

123, As a tradition, JaP, 51; cf. FoP 98

123, The one thing, FoP, 179

127, Paul is the first, MLN, 59

127, It is quite possible, JaP, 144

127, The divisions among, JaP, 144

127, The basis of the practical, JaP, 144

127, Every institution, JaP, 144

127, The learning, JaP, 145

127, All teachers, JaP, 146

128, At the very least, OFJ, 7

128, If theology, JaP, 141; cf. MLN, 57

128, The real theological issue, JaP, 142

131, In the Christian epic, CJ, 143

131, The Jesus of the parables, CJ, 144–45

131, Jesus was not merely, JNG, 19

131, The pre-eminent Christian, EF, 31

132, The word of grace, LHWG, 17–18

135, I use the term, IC, 33

135, In a canonical work, IC, 43

135, Jesus and Paul, IC, 44

136, Jesus was a strong, CJ, 162

136, The canon of Christian, IC, 33

136, To retain the New Testament, IC, 35

136, The canon of the New, HtJ, 119

136, To claim that the New, IC, 37

136, In spite of scholarly, IC, 45

137, The Christian movement, IC, 35

137, The shift to writing, IC, 36

137, The canon of the early, IC, 37

141, There is good, JaP, 110–11

141, The humanities faculty, JaP, 112

141, The spoken word, JaP, 114

142, Deans and principals, JaP, 145

142, Teachers should afford, JaP, 146

142, A reliable guide, FoP, 193

142, The professional put, TM1, 2

142, I came to see, WHA, 9

143, I weep to think, WHA, 8; cf. HtJ, 5

143, The biggest challenge, WHA, 9

143, The great thinkers, GJD

143, Universities are much, HtJ, 5

Abbreviations

BCO "Book Catalogues and Other Hyperboles"

BIG *A Beginning-Intermediate Grammar*

BRJ "Bookshelf: The Resurrection of Jesus"

CA "Commencement Address," Butler University

CaO "Creating an Opening"

Con "Conversation"

CfD "Criteria for Determining the Authentic Sayings"

CJ *A Credible Jesus*

CSS "Scholars Version"

EF "An Enlightened Faith"

EJ "The Emerging Jesus"

FfF "A Faith for the Future"

FoP *Funk on Parables*

FPC "Four-Year Political Circus"

GEW "God and the Emperor in Waco"

GJD "The Gospel of Jesus"

GoJ "The Gospel of Jesus and the Jesus of the Gospels"

HaG "Hansel & Gretel"

HDR "How Do You Read?"

HJB "How Jesus Became God"

HtJ *Honest to Jesus*

HP "The Hitching Post"

IC "The Incredible Canon"

ICr "The Incredible Creed"

IDB "The Interpreter's Dictionary of the Bible"

IHA "In the Heart of America"

IJ "The Issue of Jesus"

JA "Jesus and the Apocalypse"

JaK "Jesus and Kafka"

JaP *Jesus as Precursor*

JNG "Jesus of Nazareth: A Glimpse"

JTW "The Jesus That Was"

JVP "Jesus: A Voice Print"

LHWG *Language, Hermeneutic, and Word of God*

LL "The Second Consultation on Hermeneutics"

LSP "The Learned Society as Publisher and the University Press"

Ltr Letter, December, 17, 1993

Mem Memoir, 2002

MLN "Myth and the Literal Non-Literal"

MoM "Matters of Moment"

OFJ "The Once and Future Jesus"

PCR "Parable"

PFA "The Parables"

RBI Review of *Biblical Inspiration*, by Bruce Vawter

PRS "Press Release: Westar 1991 Spring Meeting"

SBC "Symposium on Biblical Criticism"

SBL "Society of Biblical Literature—Report of the Executive Secretary"

SME "The Sunday Morning Experience"

SP1 "Issues in Scholarly Publishing: Part 1"

SP2 "Issues in Scholarly Publishing: Part 2"

TM1 "TIME Marches On, Part 1"

TM2 "TIME Marches On, Part 2"

TT "Twenty-one Theses"

WAB "The Watershed of the American Biblical Tradition"

WHA "Where Have All the Students Gone?"

WR "The Westar Recipe"

WW "A War of Worlds"

Works Cited

Robert W. Funk

A Beginning-Intermediate Grammar of Hellenistic Greek, 3 vols. Sources for Biblical Study 2. Missoula, MT: Scholars Press, 1973.

"Book Catalogues and Other Hyperboles." *Bulletin, Council on the Study of Religion* 2 (1971), 10–22.

"Bookshelf: The Resurrection of Jesus." *The Fourth R* 8,1 (1995), 3–10.

"A Conversation of Robert Funk with John Dillenberger, James Wiggins, and Lane McGaughy. Audiotape. Santa Rosa, CA, 2002. Robert Funk Archives, Drew University Library.

"Commencement Address." [Butler University, May 2005] *The Fourth R* 19,2 (2006), 18–19.

"Creating an Opening: Biblical Criticism and the Theological Curriculum." *Interpretation* 18 (1964), 387–406.

A Credible Jesus: Fragments of a Vision. Santa Rosa, CA: Polebridge Press, 2002.

"Criteria for Determining the Authentic Sayings of Jesus." *The Fourth R* 3,6 (1990), 8–10.

"The Emerging Jesus." *The Fourth R* 2,6 (1989), 1, 11–15.

"An Enlightened Faith . . ." Pp. 17–33 in *The Future of the Christian Tradition.* Robert J. Milled, ed. Santa Rosa, CA: Polebridge Press, 2007.

"A Faith for the Future." Pp. 1–17 in *The Once & Future Faith.* Santa Rosa, CA: Polebridge Press, 2001.

"The Four-Year Political Circus: Can You Fool All the People All the Time?" *The Fourth R* 5,4 (1992), 10–12.

Funk on Parables: Collected Essays. Bernard Brandon Scott, ed. Santa Rosa, CA: Polebridge Press, 2006.

"God and the Emperor in Waco." *The Fourth R* 6,3 (1993), 14–16.

"The Gospel of Jesus and the Jesus of the Gospels." *The Fourth R* 6,6 (1993), 3–10.

"The Gospel of Jesus and the Jesus of the Gospels." Jesus Seminar, Westar Meeting, Spring 1994. DVD. Robert Funk Archives. Drew University Library.

"Hansel & Gretel, The Lone Ranger, and the Lord of the Rings." *The Fourth R* 5,5 (1992), 4–9.

"'How Do You Read?' (Luke 10:25–37)." *Interpretation* 18 (1964), 56–61.

Honest to Jesus: Jesus for a New Millennium. San Francisco: HarperSanFrancisco, 1996.

"How Jesus Became God." *The Fourth R* 4,6 (1991), 10–13.

"The Hitching Post." *Westar Magazine* 1,3 (1987), 2–3, 9.

"In the Heart of America: Redeemer Figures & Mythic Spaces." *The Fourth R* 3,4 (1990), 1–4.

"The Incredible Canon." Pp. 24–46 in *Christianity in the 21st Century.* Ed. Deborah A. Brown. New York: The Crossroad Publishing Company, 2000.

"The Incredible Creed," *The Fourth R* 10,3/4 (1997), 7–22.

"The Interpreter's Dictionary of the Bible—A Review Article." *The Drew Gateway* 34 (1964), 99–105.

"Issues in Scholarly Publishing: Part 1." *Scholarly Publishing* 9,1 (1977), 3–17.

"Issues in Scholarly Publishing: Part 2." *Scholarly Publishing* 9,2 (1978), 115–30.

"The Issue of Jesus." *Forum* 1,1 (1985), 7–12.

"Jesus and the Apocalypse." *The Fourth R* 5,2 (1992), 1–7.

"Jesus and Kafka." *CAS Faculty Journal* 1, Missoula, MT: University of Montana, 1972.

Jesus as Precursor. Revised edition. Santa Rosa, CA: Polebridge Press, 1994. Originally published as *Jesus as Precursor. Semeia* Supplements 2. Philadelphia: Fortress Press and Missoula, MT: Scholars Press, 1975.

"Jesus: A Voice Print." Pp. 9–13 in *Profiles of Jesus.* Ed. Roy W. Hoover. Santa Rosa, CA: Polebridge Press, 2002.

"Jesus of Nazareth: A Glimpse." *The Fourth R* 9,1/2 (1996), 17–20.

"The Jesus That Was." *The Fourth R* 5,6 (1992), 1–4.

Language, Hermeneutic, and Word of God: The Problem of Language in the New Testament and in Contemporary Theology. New York: Harper & Row, 1966.

"The Learned Society as Publisher and the University Press." *Bulletin, Council on the Study of Religion* 4,3 (1973), 3–13.

Letter, December, 17, 1993. Typescript. Robert Funk Archives, Drew University Library.

Memoir. 2002. Unpublished manuscript. Robert Funk Archives. Drew University Library.

"Matters of Moment: Inaugural Editorial of the *WestWord* Magazine." *Forum* 2,2 (1986), 65–68.

"Myth and the Literal Non-Literal." Pp. 57–65 in *Parable, Myth, and Language*. Edited by Tony Stoneburner. Cambridge, MA: The Church Society for College Work, 1968.

"The Once and Future Jesus." Pp. 5–25 in *The Once and Future Jesus*. Santa Rosa, CA: Polebridge Press, 1999.

"Parable." *Children's Religion* 26 (1965), 14–16.

"The Parables: A Fragmentary Agenda." Pp. 287–303 in *Jesus and Man's Hope*, vol. II. Pittsburgh Theological Seminary: A Perspective Book, 1971.

"Press Release: Westar 1991 Spring Meeting." *The Fourth R* 4,2 (1991), 1–3.

Review of *Biblical Inspiration*, by Bruce Vawter. *Journal of Ecumenical Studies* 12 (1975), 112–13.

"Scholars Version: Calling a Spade a Spade." *The Fourth R* 3,5 (1990), 12, 14.

"The Second Consultation on Hermeneutics: Logic and the Logos." *The Christian Century* 81 (1964), 1175–77.

"Society of Biblical Literature—Report of the Executive Secretary, 1968–73." *Bulletin, Council on the Study of Religion* 4,4 (1973), 8–28.

"The Sunday Morning Experience: A Codicil to Robert Price." *The Fourth R* 16,6 (2003), 15–18.

"Symposium on Biblical Criticism." *Theology Today* 33,4 (1977), 362.

"TIME Marches On, Part 1." *The Fourth R* 2,2 (1989), 1–2, 6, 8.

"TIME Marches On, Part 2." *The Fourth R* 2,3 (1989), 4–5.

"Twenty–one Theses and Notes." *The Fourth R* 11,4 (1998), 8–10.

"The Watershed of the American Biblical Tradition: The Chicago School, First Phase, 1892–1920." *Journal of Biblical Literature* 95 (1976), 4–22.

"The Westar Recipe." *Forum* NS 4,2, pp. 297–301.

"Where Have All the Students Gone?" *The Fourth R* 3,2 (1990), 8–10.

"A War of Worlds." *The Fourth R* 14,5 (2002), 6–8.